Pre-Existence

The Hidden Mystery

RICHARD FELLOWS

Copyright © 2023 Richard Fellows

PRE- EXISTENCE – THE HIDDEN MYSTERY

All rights reserved
First Published 2023

Richard Fellows reserves the right to be identified
as the author of this work.

Short extracts and brief quotations may be copied for
non-profit personal use only, without prior permission.

Otherwise, no part of this publication may be reproduced, stored in a retrieval system, or transmitted in any form or by any means, electronic, mechanical, photocopying, scanning or otherwise,
without the prior written consent of the author.

Chapter Images:	Vectorstock – vectorstock_5173190
Cover Design:	Bettina Kradolfer – www.bettinakradolfer.com

Scripture references are from the New King James Version.
Copyright © 1982 by Thomas Nelson, Inc.
Used by permission. All rights reserved.

Printed Softcover Edition: ISBN 978-0-648-58836-8

CONTENTS

PREFACE - YOU WERE THERE! 5
CHAPTER 1 - THE ORIGIN OF THE SOUL 11
CHAPTER 2 - WHAT IS MAN? 23
CHAPTER 3 - TRAGIC DAMAGE 31
CHAPTER 4 - THE ARK OF THE TESTIMONY 41
CHAPTER 5 - THE HIDDEN MYSTERY 51
CHAPTER 6 - THE ETERNAL EDEN CHURCH 61
CHAPTER 7 - THE EVIDENCE SPEAKS 67
CHAPTER 8 - COUNCIL OF RIGHTEOUS SOULS 87
CHAPTER 9 - HYMN OF THE PEARL 101
CHAPTER 10 - DIFFICULT QUESTIONS 111
CHAPTER 11 - THE VEIL OF FORGETFULNESS 119
CHAPTER 12 - MY PRIVATE GARDEN 134
CHAPTER 13 - TRANSFORMING ELOHIM 145
CHAPTER 14 - ONE STAR DIFFERS 155
CHAPTER 15 - MYSTERY STONES OF SAPPHIRES 165
CHAPTER 16 - JOB 38:7 173
CHAPTER 17 - GATHERING THOUGHTS 187
CHAPTER 18 - WOMB OF GOD 193
CHAPTER 19 - INTERPRETATIONS 203
CHAPTER 20 - THE MATRIX 211
CHAPTER 21 - ORIGEN QUOTES 223
   BIBLIOGRAPHY 230

PREFACE - YOU WERE THERE!

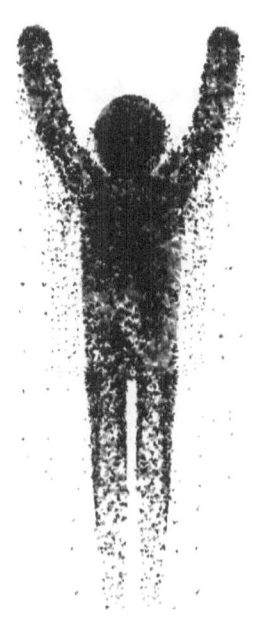

Have you ever reflected deeply on questions that concern your true identity about yourself, such as "Who" you really are? Where you really came from, and for "Why" you are here on earth. For what is a human, who are we really, and have we forgotten who we are?

William Lane Craig, in His book "Reasonable Faith" says of man quoting Loren Eiseley,

> *"Man, writes Loren Eiseley, is the Cosmic Orphan. He is the only creature in the universe who asks, "Why?" Other animals have instincts to guide them, but man has learned to ask questions. "Who am I?" he asks. "Why am I here? Where am I going?" Since the Enlightenment, when modern man threw off the shackles of religion, he has tried to answer these questions without reference to God. But the answers that have come back were not exhilarating, but dark and terrible. "You are the accidental by-product of nature, a result of matter plus time plus chance. There is no reason for your existence. All you face is death. Modern man thought that when he had gotten rid of God, he freed himself from all that repressed and stifled him. Instead, he discovered that in killing God, he had only succeeded in orphaning himself. For if there is no God, then man's life becomes absurd."*[1]

It is true that if God exists life is not absurd, but even if one believes in God and finds meaning it still does not answer the question, from where did we come "out" from, from what place, and at what stage did we receive our irrevocable callings (Rom 11:29), our gifts, talents, our scrolls of destiny (Psalm 139). Did

---

[1] William Lane Craig, Reasonable Faith; Christian Truth and Apologetics, Crossway Book Publishers, 2008, p.71

we agree to anything or did we just come into being at conception with blank minds, having to invent, chose a calling we liked once we believed and became born again.[2]

For many Christians the answer is "We are children of God", created by God from conception through our parents. But are we children of God from "conception" through our parents, or does our existence go further back, not just in God's foreknowledge, but in our essence back into eternity. Some would say, God "adds" the "soul" instantaneously at conception, which begs the question, does God create a sinful, corrupt soul in a fallen body to be born? If we push the explanation a little further one may say, the soul exists created, seconds before entering the body (apart from it), pure to begin with. But this concludes then, that we existed before conception, and if this is the case, how far back did we exist in eternity, seconds, or a period of eternal time?

Christians have generally believed,

* God has foreknowledge of who will exist from eternity from His mind, and it is these that will come into being at conception through parents.

* The "soul" was created seconds before conception, pure, then inserted to avoid the logic of God instantaneously creating the soul at conception making God the creator of a corrupt soul in a fallen body.

There has been in history heated debates about the soul's origin, and this has produced three main positions (these we will look at more deeply in a later chapter), these are,

---

[2] Are are callings and talents just preprogramed into us, and we sense them for the first time in the earth or did we agree to them in Heaven and then sense them in the earth from pre-imprints of memories and ordinations from above?

* **Creationism** - that the soul is created at conception.

* **Traducian** - that the soul is created indirectly through parents. Both soul and body are generated by father and mother. The soul comes from the sperm and ovum only.

* **Pre-existence** - that the soul has existed before conception and in the past in eternity (not eternal itself, but created and lived in eternity with God first).

I believe that the first two have seriously problems, from logic and the Scriptures, and Jewish Theology.

I believe we don't just come into the world with a blank slate of a mind. I believe we have forgotten our true origin, seeing dimly in the mirror, while being in a darkened world, a fallen world. That is before this world we did see fully in the mirror of our true self and identity in the light of God, seeing God as He is known.

> *"For now we see in a mirror dimly, but then face to face. Now I know in part, but then I shall know just as I also am known." (1 Corinthians 13:12)*

As we will see in later chapters, Jewish Theology, Jewish traditions say, that when our soul leaves heaven to come to earth, an angel taps our face and our memories of Paradise fade to a spark.

In forgetting, we replace the dimly seen world to be our guide of understanding and in our sin natures we lose our true reality. We were there in eternity in hidden treasuries, a hidden mystery in the secret place (Psalm 91:1-2).

When a soul is sent to earth and is born it awakes to a dim shadow of recollection. The soul has a spark of remembrance, a restless longing for the eternity written in its heart, for the place it knows, but cannot see. It is only once we are born again and revelation starts to fill our souls, and our spirit's see clearer, that we understand our true self and destiny.

Jesus hinted that things (souls) were hidden before the creation of the world.

> *Jesus spoke, 'all these things to the crowd in parables; he did not say anything to them without using a parable. So was fulfilled what was spoken through the prophet; 'I will open my mouth in parables, I will utter things hidden since the creation of the world." (Matthew 13:34-35)*

Jesus said, he would utter things since the creation of the world. He spoke of the "mystery" of the Kingdom of God. A mystery is a truth that is unknown by men and women in the earth apart from divine revelation.

> *"The knowledge of the secrets of the Kingdom of God has been given to you, but to others I speak in parables, so that, through seeing, they may not see, thou hearing they may not understand." (Luke 8:9-10)*

Jesus spoke to awaken our memory of the mystery, a secret only for us because we were in the secret place. The mystery that was ordained before the ages for our glory (1 Cor 2:7). We were there, we are the unfolding mystery from before the creation of the world. To those in the hidden treasury he told ineffable mysteries, and he taught unspeakable doctrines to all those who became the children of light.

> *"Shepherd of the sheep, through the blood of the everlasting covenant' (Hebrews 13:20)*

> *"The everlasting Gospel" (Revelation 16:4)*

This knowledge that we have pre-existed brings forth some beautiful revelation. It means that God has already really loved us and cared for us above. That we have already had fellowship with the Father, Son and Holy Spirit, and have looked into the mirror of our full "image" fully loved.[3]

In this book, we will be doing a study of our pre-existence in Christ from before the foundation of the world (Eph 1:3). Before we enter this study and journey, I will first explain the methodology taken in revealing the revelation. I will make the case that we lived in heaven before being sent to earth by using the Holy Scriptures of the Bible. I will also quote many extra-biblical ancient Jewish texts that confirm the Scriptures. As the Book of Enoch was accepted by many of the early Church Fathers[4], if a truth is stated in the Book of Enoch, and I find the same truth in other books, things stated, I will also quote from them bringing multiply witnesses. I will also quote from Jewish Rabbis, Jewish traditions, and the early Church Fathers.

---

[3] You may also find that this truth of pre-existence reshapes your understanding of Predestination.

[4] This will be documented in a later Chapter!

CHAPTER 1 - THE ORIGIN OF THE SOUL

In this Chapter, we will be looking at the nature of the origin of the soul, and how this has been explained throughout early Church history. One should note, and this will be covered in a later chapter, the Jewish position is very clear (pre-existence), and as we will see in that later chapter, it is extensively documented. It seems very strange to me why the Church didn't follow the majority[5] view of the origin of the soul. But for now, we will deal with the debate that has gone on in the Church.

There are three primary views on the origin of the soul that have been held by Christians. They are the Pre-existence view, the Creationism view, and the Traducian view. The pre-existent view is what I favour, but it's not popular, but also, I don't think it is explained clearly either which doesn't help. But before we start examining the views, we must understand that the word *"soul and spirit"* can be used in terms as meaning kind of the same thing, and also as being different from each other. A bit like the sun's essence is different from its rays. They are the same in the sense that they are immaterial, but different in that one unfolds from the other. That is why Scripture talks about the spirit, soul and body. Three aspects, but can be described as two often by many, for example, we have a spirit, but once it has entered into the body we form soulish emotions, a soul realm unfolds, and once in the body, the soul is a faculty of the body.

The Pre-existent view holds, that our soul pre-existed in heaven first and came out of God to be sent into a body. The Christian view is not the Platonic (Greek) view describing that the soul is eternal and uncaused. The Christian view is that the soul was created, came forth from God and abided in heaven first under the throne in the "Treasury of Souls" until it's appointed time to be sent. Each human being's body is generated

---

[5] When I say majority, I'm talking about Jewish beliefs and other cultures held to it.

by his parents, and at conception the soul is sent from above into the embryo.

The Creationism view holds, that God directly creates a new individual soul for everyone born into this world. While the body of each new human being is generated by his or her parents through the natural process, the soul is supernaturally created by God at conception. The soul at conception simply comes into existence simultaneous with human conception (egg and sperm). But did not come from heaven before, but was created on the spot.

The Traducian view holds, that the soul is created indirectly through parents. Both soul and body are generated by father and mother and that the soul comes from the sperm and ovum only.

Some arguments against Pre-existence; the scientific evidence points to individual human life beginning at conception. If they were brought into being at a point of time, then they have not existed from eternity. Problem with this is "Science" only picks up what is happening at the materialistic realm, and not before, so how can it rule out what is happening before. Also saying that a soul appeared at a point of time, first in heaven or on earth, does not mean a created soul in a realm of time, (point of time) cannot first exist in eternity, itself not being eternally uncaused. I mean angels were created in heaven at a point of time, but are not uncaused.

Some arguments against Creationism; some say a soul appearing on the spot at conception does not escape the charge of the inheritance of original sin (we with deal with the same argument for pre-existence later). For would a perfect God create a fallen soul[6] in a material body? I would say no, but a perfect God could create a pure soul in heaven and send it to enter a damage

---

[6] That is every soul after the fall of Adam and Eve is born into a fallen world.

creation from the misuse of creature freedom.[7] The creation view also holds that God is continually creating souls, but God finished creating back in Genesis 2:3, He doesn't create any more, He sends, moulds, and sustains creation now.

Some arguments against Traducian; if all souls are in the loins or wombs of their parents only, then if a person dies, do all the souls that were in them die, and are these now not able to be born? Does mankind control who comes into the world ultimately? I would say NO! Even if God put all souls in Adam first and souls flow from transmission instead of God being the sole origin, man is still controlling the destiny of the world. Also, how can an immaterial soul be passed down through a material process? Yes, to be born you have to have parents, to be born involves the act of sex, but does the man or woman if they die cut off many souls from being born that somehow live in their bodies, whole generations? Eve was not conceived from Adam's sperm or through sex, so where did her soul come from? Same problem of original sin, the soul is created fallen.

Another question can be asked, and many ask it, "Why", was I even born? Born because of random sex into existence without an ultimate purpose. Yes, sex can be for procreation, planned and unplanned, and sometimes just for pleasure. Were we born without a purpose, without a mission? The pre-existence view, ordains a reason you were born, God was in control, God ordained you with a mission and purpose written.

The pre-existent view is not as senseless as many think. God created all souls in heaven and placed them in the "Treasury of Souls" under the throne to be sent in/at their appointed time, with a reason and purpose and mission for their lives. The spirit (soul) is sent in God's timing through the second cause (sex) of

---

[7] Creature freedom includes all created beings, angels and humans.

a "parent and parent" act of conception (covenant of love) and an immaterial soul is fused into a material body and grows until born. God being perfect, sends an unfallen soul into a damaged fallen creation body, He did not create a fallen soul/body on the spot. Also God is in control of who is born. If the Traducian view was true, if marry died when she was a baby, the Messiah would never have been born as God couldn't have chosen another vessel.

As the soul enters a fallen world, it is influenced by the world, and its make up, and the body it lives in. It enters a damaged world, a damaged body, some more damaged than others. Look at beautiful handicap children or brain damaged children, an "out-come" of a fallen creation. Choice exists in heaven, one can sin in heaven (though souls haven't), but you will be thrown out like the angels did if you do. Souls in heaven haven't fallen, but when they are sent to earth, the trials and testing s start and like Adam and Eve; they fall and their consciousness and structure of DNA in their bodies become fallen in sin, scarred and damaged affecting future generations, both soul and body. They become slaves to a nature, that was once good, that has now become a salve to a sin nature, which sin now affects and tempts the inner desires until born again. From Adam all souls are affected, not guilty for what Adam did, but damaged from it, born in it and are held responsible for their actions, from their sinful desires- "For we are judged according to the deeds done in the body" (2 Cor 5:10, Rom 2:6. Col 3:25). Every soul born in the world cannot save itself, its damage is too strong, it must be born again.

The Christian Apologist Paul Copan, says in his Book, 'Loving Wisdom; Christian Philosophy of Religion',

> *"Our deeply sinful condition should be understood as the damage or consequences of Adam fall, not his guilt. The position seems both biblically accurate and much less morally problematic. Being in sin - a given condition from birth, indeed, from conception is different from sinning, for which we're responsible and which renders us guilty and blameworthy. We're born with an original corruption, a self-centred orientation that permeates all we do. But simply being born or conceived in sin (Psalm 51:5) doesn't render a human guilty before God. While we can accept original sin, the damage view, original guilt seems morally troublesome."*[8]

We all died in Adam, as we were all separated by a condition of sin. We are all a family and "family acts" have consequences for all. Despite the charge of unfairness that Adam ruined things for everyone else, it could well be God knew that any of us human beings over time, in the testing environment on earth would have freely disobeyed in the garden.[9]

It is the misuse of freedom, enhanced by the damage of our fallen "state of being", with our damaged DNA of our "image" that we have become broken orphans, reinforcing evil into our consciousness making it stronger and stronger until we are born again, and set free from our damaged nature. Yes, the sin nature does exist from a damaged reality. And, yes, we are also slaves to sin until we are fully redeemed, but this does not make us guilty of Adam's sin.

The view of pre-existence was not held by many of the early Church Fathers, but it was held by a number of them, which is normally not mentioned in this debate (these will be docu-

---

[8] Paul Copan, Loving Wisdom, Christian Philosophy of Religion, Chalice Press, 2007, p. 140
[9] Copan, p.144

mented in a later chapter). It was at the Fifth Ecumenical Council that took place in Constantinople in 553 AD, (also known as the Second Council of Constantinople), where 165 bishops under Pope Vigilius and Emperor Justinian made a ruling that the idea of the pre-existence of the soul was wrong and almost worthy of being damned. What is strange about this is just about every ancient Jewish text believes in the pre-existence of the soul. Rabbi's and Jewish traditions believe the soul is pre-existent, and hold that the other views are based in Greek philosophy. It is a fact that one can find early Church Fathers for the first 400 years of the Church believing in the doctrine of pre-existence.

As I said in the Preface, as part of my methodology, I will be using the Book of Enoch and many other ancient Jewish texts. If many in the Church for the first 500 years believed in the reliability of the Book of Jubilees and the Book of Enoch (and others), then it's not so simple to just reject the doctrine of pre-existence, and also these councils are not infallible.

For now, in this chapter, as an example I will just use two references, from the Book of Jubilees and the Book of Enoch, and show that the Church trusted these books, even calling the Book of Enoch Scripture, and these books document pre-existence.

The Book of Jubilees is an ancient Jewish text from the Second Temple period. As a text, it played a significant role in the religion of the first century AD. Josephus made heavy use of it in his Antiquities. Many of the ideas found in Jubilees appear in the New Testament, casually mixed as traditions with the text of the Hebrew Scriptures themselves. In a handful of places, the New Testament authors seem to cite Jubilees directly.

Witness to the Book of Enoch[10],

Epistle of Jude - quotes a section of 1 Enoch 1:9 which is a Midrash of Deuteronomy 33:2 as "the seventh from Adam, prophesied" (1 Enoch 1:9). "Seventh from Adam," Enoch, identifies him as the author, Adam's fifth great-grandson and thus Noah's great-grandfather. Many commentators on Jude have noted that Jude uses the dative "prophesied to these" (τούτοις, toutois) and not the normal "concerning these". "Prophesied" means that Jude is not simply quoting an historical fact, but that Enoch gave a prophecy, which by definition is an utterance from God. The following verses in Jude develop further material from the named book.

Epistle of Barnabas - (ca 70 AD – 132 AD) quotes Enoch as "Scripture", sometimes with the formula "it is written."

Justin Martyr- (110 AD – 165 AD), in his Second Apology, uses information unique to the Book of Enoch to establish doctrine on fallen angels and the origin of demons from angels' adultery with women.

Athenagoras - (133 AD – 190 AD) in his Plea for the Christians uses Enoch to establish doctrine about Genesis 6:1-4, calling Enoch a prophet: "you know that we say nothing without witnesses, but state the things which have been declared by the prophets."

---

[10] https://en.wikipedia.org/wiki/Reception_of_the_book_of_Enoch_before_modern_times

Irenaeus - (d. 202 AD), in Against Heresies, discusses the doctrine that Enoch was God's legate to fallen angels, which is unique to Enoch, and that a group of fallen angels devised methods of sorcery to adulterate with women.

Clement of Alexandria - (ca 150 AD – ca 215 AD) writes that both Daniel and Enoch taught the same thing regarding the blessing of the faithful (Eclogue 2.1) and that the fallen angels were the source of the black arts (53.4).

Tertullian- (155 AD – 222 AD), the first author writing in Latin, names and cites Enoch as "divinely inspired" in On the Apparel of Women (Book I) and names Enoch as its genuine, human author. He states that its quotation in Jude 14 is an attestation in the New Testament to its authenticity, though he notes that it is "not received by some, because it is not admitted into the Jewish canon either". He writes— But since Enoch in the same Scripture has preached likewise concerning the Lord, nothing at all must be rejected by us which pertains to us; and we read that "every Scripture suitable for edification is divinely inspired" (2 Tim 3:16). By [non-believers] it may now seem to have been rejected for that very reason, just like all the other passages which plainly tell of Christ.

In Book II, Tertullian uses Enoch to establish doctrine against the excessive ornamentation of women, attributing its origin to demons who cohabitated with them before the Great Flood.

Within his Apologetic, in *On Idolatry*, he uses Enoch to establish the doctrine that idolatry and astrology originated from demons and that demons are the supernatural issue of fallen angels adulterating with women.

Anatolius - (early 3rd c AD – July 3, 283 AD) cites Enoch to interpret the ancient Jewish calendar (in a reference to Enoch, Book of Starlight).

Cassiodorus - (ca 485 AD – ca 585 AD), quotes Jude 14 ("In these words he (Jude) verifies the prophecy") to verify Enoch's prophecy as contained in 1 Enoch. In the same Latin translation of comments on the First Epistle of Peter attributed to Clement of Alexandria (ca.150 – 211/216), Cassiodorus also uses Enoch to establish doctrine that fallen angels are apostates from God.

Syncellus - (d. p̄ 810 AD), who once held a position of authority under the patriarch Tarasios of Constantinople, quotes numerous excerpts of the book of Enoch in his Chronography.

The Book of Jubilees says,

"On the first day of creation, God made, "all of the spirits of His creatures, which minister before Him, several angelic beings, and all of the spirits of His creatures that are in Heaven and on earth." (2 Cen C.E)

The Book of Enoch!

1 Enoch 62:7-8 - describes the Son of Man together with the congregation of the Elect before their sowing in the earth.

"All souls are prepared for eternity, before the composition of the earth." (2 Enoch 23)

1 Enoch 70:4 says, 'He saw the fathers of the righteous who from the beginning dwelt in that place'.

And I swear to you, that there has been no man in his mother's womb, but that already before, even to each one there is a place prepared for repose of the soul, and a measure fixed how much it is intended that a man be tried in this world. Yea children, deceive not yourselves, for there has been previously prepared a place for every soul of man." (2 Enoch 49:3)

In 3 Enoch (Hebrew Enoch), Rabbi Ishmael, the recipient of the vision, is shown the spirits of the righteous who are yet to be born (3 Enoch 43:1)[11]

---

[11] Yes, 3 Enoch is written at a much later date than the others and not by Enoch, but is added as it follows the others in thought.

CHAPTER 2 - WHAT IS MAN?

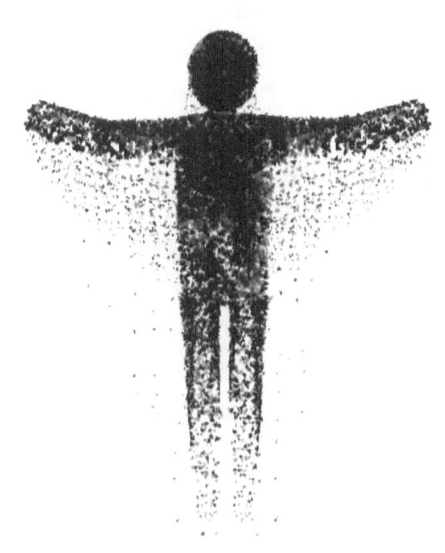

Following on from the debate of the origin of the soul, in this Chapter, we will look at the question of, 'What is man?', and its explanation in revealing who we are. What is man in his fullness, an ape, a created dust man, or a "formed" flesh body (house) to hold and reveal the mystery of the image of God[12]. Man reflects the Trinity, that is in spirit, body, and glory, in the pattern of the journey of the eternal Son, but on a created level (not uncaused). Our true identity is we are a kind of *'elohim'*, a son (daughter) of God. We came out of God in glory as created spirit's (sons of God, different than the angels) and were sent to earth into flesh bodies to be resurrected in to glorious bodies, tested and refined, walking by faith, while seeing dimly in a fallen world to triumph over evil.

As a created elohim, we lived in the "Treasury of Souls" sanctuary under the throne, and under the headship of Christ, as being His body, members of the royal house-hold of God, chosen in Him from before the foundation of the world[13]. This is where we looked into the full mirror of the image of God, God Himself, and lived in His love. It is here that we were given our irrevocable callings and instructions in the secret place under the shadow of His wings.

Now, God is the eternal Elohim (uncreated- Trinity), but there are also lower elohim. Angels are called elohim, and they are different to God, and different to us (humans). They are in some sense an elder race to us, but different. We are not angels, but they are part of the family of God. Humans are created in

---

[12] The mystery being our spirit, soul and body fully mirroring the image of God.

[13] Ephesians 1:4 - and 2nd century text the Hymn of the Pearl says, 'When I was a little child I was nurtured in the royal house of my Father, my Mother, Queen of the East, and the second in command, Jesus Christ, with loving care in the midst of abundance and glory.'

the "image and likeness of God", but Scripture does speak, giving an example of the deceased Samuel in the original text, as an "elohim" (says Biblical Scholar Michael Heiser[14]) - (modern translation puts spirit) (1 Sam 28:13). It is also stated that we were created a little lower than the angels, different from them, but will be exalted above them, and judge them. We also have that difficult verse where Jesus addresses the leaders in the council on earth, saying "didn't I say to you, You are gods (elohim)"[15].

There are many "beings" who hold the term Elohim. God is called Elohim, but no other elohim is like Him. There are many lower elohim, and all are part of the house hold of God.

Michael Heiser in his Book "The Unseen Realm" says,

> *"The Old Testament writers understand that Yahweh was an elohim, but no other elohim was Yahweh. He was species-unique among all residents of the spiritual world. The word "elohim" is a phase of residence, it has nothing to do with a specific set of attributes."*

There are a number of Scriptures that affirm that we have a spirit (soul) of which came down from heaven,

- *"Every good gift and every perfect gift is from above, and comes down from the Father of lights, with whom there is no variation or shadow or turning."* (Jam 1:17)

- Father God created all spirits in eternity, because He is our Father - *"Further, we have had human fathers who corrected us, and we paid them respect. Shall we*

---

[14] Michael S. Heiser, The Unseen Realm, Lexham Press, 2015, p.30
[15] A number of early Church Fathers said, that humans were to become gods (Justin Martyr, Tertullian, Irenaeus, and others). And a number cited Psalm 82, referring that it spoke of humans as gods (Justin Martyr, Irenaeus, Methodius, Hyppolytus, Theophilus and others). These are documented in later Chapters. Also the Scriptures teach the doctrine of Theosis.

not much more readily be in subjection to the Father of spirits and live?" (Heb 12:9).

- *"God the Judge of all, to the spirits of just men made perfect."* (Heb 12:23)

- *"Therefore, since we are the offspring of God..."* (Acts 17:29)

- God chose a family to be in Christ before the foundation of the world (Eph 1:4)

- God showed Abram his descendants in the sky, hinting at 'stars' that would come to earth (Gen 15:5)

- *"Thus says the Lord, who stretches out the heavens, lays the foundation of the earth, and forms the spirit of man within him."* (Zec 12:1)

- When we were sent our pre appointed time was determined, *"every nation of men to dwell on all the face of the earth, and has determined their pre-appointed times and the boundaries of their dwellings."* (Acts 17:26)

- *Jesus said, 'As You sent me into the world, I also have sent them into the world.'* (John 17:18)

- *"And the Lord God formed man of the dust of the ground, and breathed into his nostrils the breath (spirit) of life, and man became a living being."* (Gen 2:7)

- *"Then the dust will return to the earth as it was. And the spirit will return to God who gave it."* (Ecc 12:7)

- *"Who knows the spirit of the sons of men, which goes upward..."* (Ecc 3:21) - back to where it came.

> *"What is man that You should exalt him. That You should set your heart upon him." (Job 7:17)*

One must ask, "Why", is it that God is mindful of man', it is because He has set His heart upon him, His eternal LOVE! and has written eternity in his heart as he reflects the eternal image of God. We came forth from that love, in that love, and out of that love having been loved eternally. It is written in our heart for it is the stamp of our home.

> *"For You have made him a little lower than the angels, and You crowned him with glory and honor" (Psalm 8:5)*

If spirit's (souls) existed in heaven first as much evidence points to this, and our "being", "essence", spirit, is a copy of God's image and glory, then we were crowned with glory and honour before the foundation of the world. Adam's Spirit was sent and God then breathed into his dust body in the garden and he became a living being. His spirit of glory shone through his body and shined all around him, that being his; soul/spirit and body was glorious. Then after the fall his glory faded back into his body unable to shine through his corrupted state[16].

To say our spirit is not part of the reflection of the image of God, the glory of God is to say we were not glorious in heaven or crowned with glory and honour. Like-wise to say our spirit just appeared in a body at the same time, at once, at conception,

---

[16] The human body literally glows, emitting a visible light in extremely small quantities at levels that rise and fall with the day, it's just too dim for our weak eyes to pick up on, scientists now reveal. Research has shown that the body emits visible light, 1,000 times less intense than the levels to which our naked eyes are sensitive. In fact, virtually all living creatures emit very weak light. (This visible light differs from the infrared radiation — an invisible form of light — that comes from body heat.).
https://www.nbcnews.com/id/wbna32090918

on the spot, into existence from nowhere is to say God created a fallen soul - being!

As for us "We" were sent to earth, but our spirit of glory is blocked to shine through our bodies fully because of the fall of creation and its damaging effects. We were crowned with glory, but we have lost some of our honour from the fall of creation. We are now in fallen bodies, as fallen humanity. As we grow up in the earth and look into a mirror, and reflect on "Who" we are we see ourselves dimly in the mirror. Like getting out of the shower and looking in the mirror and it's all misty. We do not see the fullness of who we are, we are a mystery to be revealed. But the mystery already existed, it's not just something we add to in the future. That mystery is we pre-existed in heaven, but due to our corrupt state, we do not see ourselves as we "fully" are.

> *"For now, **we see in a mirror dimly**, but then face to face. Now **I** know **in** part; then **I** shall know fully, even as **I** have been fully known." (1 Corinthians 13:12)*

We see dimly because we are separated from God and our spirit is shut down (due to corruption and our sin nature) to a low degree of vibration from our fallen state to receive fellowship with God, unable until we are born again. We can grasp God, but cannot have intimate fellowship until we are born again.

> *"So that they should seek the Lord, in the hope that they might grope for Him and find Him, though He is not far from each one of us." (Acts 17:27)*

Our spirit's in coming to earth are made to forget our past experiences in heaven, so that we can focus on the pilgrimage on earth, focus on the testings, the trials, the overcoming of evil choices, and to learn the way of love as well as living with the mundane of times. Our ultimate objective is to be born again, and realise who we really are, a transforming elohim.

So, as we close this Chapter, lets recap some truths 1. We are separated from God by the damage of the fall on creation and its effect on our corrupt bodies making us dead in fellowship to God (a slave to sin). 2. Our spirit is shut down by the fall to know God fully, and He has put a veil over our minds so that we don't remember our time in heaven. But God does not wipe out the knowledge of Himself for He is clearly seen in creation (Rom 1:20), just the knowledge of our pre-experiences.

If we are created in the image of God first above then we already at one point (in heaven when we came forth from God) had the full glory, unless you say we were less than the image of God to start with. On earth we are being redeemed back to God's full glory. We can't have been created less than God's glory to become His image. No, we were in His image from the start and are being restored. The mystery before will be lived out to reveal who we really are. But we are still responsible to walk worthy as one star will shine brighter than another in glory.

> *"But we all with unveiled face, beholding as in a mirror the glory of the Lord, are be transformed into the same image from glory to glory, just by the spirit of the Lord." (2 Corinthians 3:18)*

CHAPTER 3 - TRAGIC DAMAGE

In the last Chapter, we looked at the nature of our true identity, and our separation from God. In this Chapter, we will reflect on the effect that the fall has had on our function in the world, and in seeing the Kingdom and its presence.

We will start with Adam,

Adam's body was formed from the dust of the ground, and God breathed His spirit into Adam. God breathed, and sent Adam's spirit body in its "perfect" state of glory from heaven, to step into his earthy flesh; body-casing house. Adam's spirit body shone through his body and clothed him with glory. The expression of God's image, united in Adam's unique reflection of glory was his temple body on earth. When Adam's spirit body entered his earthy body his consciousness and spiritual senses were plugged into his flesh body and soul faculties, and were joined to work as one. The soul is a faculty of the fleshly body to sense and feel the earth realm. We are made up of a spirit, a soul realm and a body.

We have a spirit body and a soul that acts in our body. I take the spirit and soul to be the same thing, but once the spirit is in the body there is an entangling and out of our spirit; a realm manifests with soul emotions in the body. As the spirit/soul enters the body there is a realm that manifests with earthly emotions and feelings and is independent in the body. The spirit/soul is different than the 'soul realm' so when you come across me talking about the soul realm, it is a realm in the body that has been produced from the spirit/soul.

When Adam was created, he was created good, his intrinsic nature was good. Then Eve was created from Adam's side and the two reflected God's image on earth in the garden, both clothed in glory.

When Adam and Eve sinned their glory covering was affected, it stained their conscience and they were morally out of alignment. Their spirit body faded with its glory and was separated from its relationship with the newly formed realm of earthy feelings. The spirit's awareness of heaven and many of its abilities were shut down and their functioning was distorted.

Our "eyes are the window of our souls", but also our "soul realm" is a window (connection) to our spirit-body. Before the fall, Adam's spirit shone through with glory and perfection with heavenly awareness of eternity, enlightening his earthy emotions & desires. After the fall this was shut down greatly.

When Adam and Eve fell their conscience was darkened and their DNA was damaged (and they started to slowly die)[17]. The glory they had faded and their soul realm like a window became dirty and darkened. Their soul realms were stained with sin, and the strength and power of awareness from their spirit was dimly shut down in degree. They were uncovered naked, un-clothed of glory as their perfect spirits of glory withdrew back into their bodies. The dimness of their spirit's shut down their deep fellowship, and they were separated from God.[18]

---

[17] Adam was warned in Genesis 2:17 that if he ate of the 'Tree of the Knowledge of Good and Evil' he would die. Adam must of had access to the Divine Council before he lost his immortality. - "Who can climb to the heavens and become immortal? Only a member of the Divine Assembly live forever." (Gilgamesh Tablet III). Adam lost immortality, and we will regain it - "For this corruptible must put on incorruption, and this mortal must put on immortality. So when this corruptible shall have put on incorruption, and this mortal shall have put on immortality, then shall be brought to pass the saying that is written, Death is swallowed up in victory." (1 Cor 15:53-54).

[18] Psalm 8:5, says, 'For you have made him a little lower than the angels, and have crowned him with glory and honor." - 'When God created me out of the earth along with Eve your Mother, I used to go about here in glory which, she had seen in the aeon from which we had come.' (Apocalypse of Adam) - Church Father Chrysostom 380 AD, 'While sin and disobedience had not yet come on

They had died spiritually, not in the sense their spirit was dead, but was so dimly shut down corrupted by the soul realm that they were "dead" in fellowship, separated, cut off from God and His awareness, and their awareness of where they had come from. Even after the fall, God could still come to them, but they were to be cut off. For God said, where are you Adam after the fall and he answered, but this was because God called, showed up in His presence first.

From the fall every "spirit" (child) that enters the womb, enters fallen bodies, and their perfect spirit is encased in fallen, damaged DNA. Our spirit has an influence over our own individuality, it is our blueprint, and also takes on traits from our parents. The spirit enters the womb, the matrix of the world and is born seeing dimly. Every spirit born has the same issue as Adam - the strength of their spirit is low, alive, but so dim it is separated from God in a deadness of fellowship.

This dimness and corruption damage that we are born into from the fall affects every aspect of our being. It affects, it does not kill or eradicate it. It affects the mind, it is darkened (Rom 3:11), the will is twisted (2 Peter 2:19), and affections are disordered (Isa 57:21, Titus 3:3,1 Pet 2:11). All relationships are distorted, stained, or broken, both with God (Gen 3:8-10) and with others (Jas 4:1-2). Humans are morally evil, spiritually sick, spiritually blind, lost in bondage to sin, and live under a sentence of physical death and spiritual separation until born again.

All that are born have fallen short of the glory of God, but this "fallenness" has degrees of which humans can harden even

---

the scene, they were clad in glory from above which caused them no shame. But after the breaking of the law, then entered the scene both shame and awareness of their nakedness. Church Father Ephraem, 400 AD,'It is because of the glory with which they were clothed that they were not ashamed. When it was taken away from them after they violated the commandment, they were indeed ashamed, because they were naked.'

more, and entangle oneself into great wounds and demonic bondage (Yes, we can make it worse). In early times, many people cut off from God, worshipped false gods, and because of their knowledge of a spiritual world could encounter spiritual dimensions and demonic powers. As people lived on, mindsets were changed and people's perceptions drew away from the gods and just believed in a materialistic world (atheism), for them their "fallenness" of the knowledge of the world has gone to a deeper degree. Their minds have lost perceptions of reality, that do exist, but they don't see from their hardness. Our perceptions from the lens of sin affects how we interpret the world.

There are a number of reasons why people don't believe in God,

* From our fallenness- we are separated from His presence and our natures resist due to sin.

* From our perceptions we interpret reality wrongly.

* From the dimness of our spirit's - we are alienated from God - But while being dim, it does not eradicate all awareness. Acts 17:27 of the fallen nature says- "So that they should seek the Lord in the hope that they might grope for Him and find Him, though He is not far from each one of us." Romans 1:20 says that the mature are accountable and are without excuse for God has made His invisible attributes seen in the things He has made.

* In our fallenness, the more wounded we get, damaged, scarred in our souls the more entangled we are to destructive ways.

* From being in a fallen world, not only do we have our own problems, we have principalities that blind us and

others with demonic ideas, and can control them and possess them.

Once a soul (child) is in the earth apart from having their parents, they still have an orphan spirit, we all have an orphan spirit unless we are born again and connected to our Father in heaven. This orphan spirit leads many in destructive ways and entangles their souls in sin. While being an unbeliever they are under the sway of the devil, rejected and under the father of lies, until born again to connect to their heavenly creator Father. But even then, some believers still live with orphan spirit's because they do not address their wounds and untangle from destructive ways and sanctify.

We should also note that "fallenness" or one who is not born again, does not mean that they cannot "SEE" or encounter the Kingdom of God, or rub up against it. Yes, John 3:3 says, "Most assuredly, I say to you, unless one is born again, he cannot see the Kingdom of God." - but this must be read in context. One can encounter the Kingdom, but not belong to the Kingdom.

To "see" the Kingdom here means to belong to the Kingdom, to be part of it, to enter and see and live in heavenly realms. It does not mean unless you are born again you cannot have any awareness of the Kingdom's existence.

For example - A friend was doing battle against a witch, and as the battle increased each day, light from the Kingdom shone brighter and brighter into the witch's house and she got weaker and weaker and sick, that she had to stop her magic attacks and hand over ground. The witch encountered a stronger Kingdom.

The occult knows of the spiritual world, and they would see angels of the Kingdom many times doing battle with them.

Another example - a journalist was sitting on a seat on a campus that lived under an open heaven. The journalist was a first-time visitor and was an atheist. When she was about to leave, she could not get off her seat, she said, 'there was a presence so strong on her that she couldn't get up'. She encountered the Kingdom.

So being in a fallen state does not mean you cannot know the spiritual world is real or that one cannot rub up against the Kingdom's reality. What it does mean is due to our sin nature and dim spirit's, we resist the knowledge of the Kingdom.

Young children often can encounter the Kingdom because their spirits are soft and God's spirit can just come upon them without having to shift great wounds hardened in the soul realm. Also many babies and children can be born again and encounter, just like John, as he had the spirit while he was in his mother's womb.

Handicap people can encounter the Kingdom and be saved sovereignly by God, because they are not morally accountable due to not being mentally rational. The age of accountability kicks in. Scripture says, we are Judged according to "moral deeds done in the flesh". As long as God saves in His justice and mercy and covers their fallenness and damaged nature they will be saved.

In the fall the glory of God faded on all creation as well, and it seems that if one lives under an open heaven, the intensity of God's presence and glory takes over the fallen atmosphere (environment) and rules over it and affects anyone who visits. The glory over powers their fallen souls, and adds to the strength of their dim spirits to encounter.

On earth in our bodies, we can encounter heaven, our spirit bodies can travel and appear in heaven (Paul did), but we also have a soul realm cord in our bodies. Our soul is to be sanctified and transformed on earth, and when we die, one day our body will be restored to a resurrected body of glory. We have a spirit body of glory, and we will have a resurrected body of glory as one.

As I said above, even believers who are born again, and their spirits are plugged into their soul realm, and are in fellowship with God can still live with orphan characters. Their spirit is plugged in, they are born again, saved, a new creation, joined as spirit, soul and body, but the light and Spirit of God must wash us as we yield in being sanctified. As we yield to God's spirit, our spirit shines brighter into our soul realm, and our wounds and sin's get untangled. This is how we go from glory to glory. Some believers stay as orphans, others stay in deep sin, and this will be seen in heaven as one star (talking of us) differs from another in glory, some will shine brighter than others.

> *"Let us lay aside (yield) every weight, and the sin which so easily entangles us, and let us run with endurance the race set before us." (Hebrews 12:1)*

Our understanding of life begins in heaven. There the spirit children of God were taught his eternal plan for their destiny. It has also been decreed by God that spirit's upon taking bodies, shall forget all they had known previously, or they could not have a day of trial, could not have an opportunity for proving themselves in darkness and temptation, in unbelief and wickedness, to prove themselves worthy of eternal existence. When we were sent to earth and God placed us here, He put a veil of forgetfulness on our previous existence, so that we might experience a time of testing, an opportunity to prove ourselves and qualify for all that God has prepared for us to receive. To obtain perfection, we had to leave our pre-earth home and come to earth. During the transfer, a veil was drawn over our spiritual eyes, and the memory of our premortal experiences was suspended.

This veil as the border between mortality and eternity; it is also a film of forgetting which covers the memories of earlier experiences. This forgetfulness will be lifted one day, and on that day, we will see forever--rather than "through a glass darkly" (1 Cor. 13:12). We are cocooned, as it were, in order that we might truly choose. Once, long ago, we chose to come to this very setting where we could choose. It was an irrevocable choice! And the veil is the guarantor that our ancient choice is honoured. We are clearly not at home in time--because we belong to eternity!

When we are born into this world, we only have a vague recollection of our pre-existent life. By the inspiration of the Spirit "we see through a glass dimly" and we "know in part." Ultimately our previous knowledge will be restored to us when that which is perfect comes, and then we shall know even as also we are known.

A Jewish teaching says, God sits in a circle with many baby spirits that are about to be born. God knows that the babies won't experience the same joy on earth that they experienced in heaven, and He doesn't want them to be dissatisfied. So, God touches His finger just below their noses leaving an indentation on their upper lips. This makes them forget the joys of Heaven, so that they can adapt to the world into which they are born. When it is a time for a spirit to be born, angels bring us into the womb.[19]

---

[19] Howard Schwartz, Tree of Souls, Oxford University Press, 2004, p.140

CHAPTER 4 - THE ARK OF THE TESTIMONY

We came forth from God, out of the Fathers words like a vibration, manifesting through the womb of the Holy Spirit, to sit under the headship of the eternal Son. As spirits from the eternal Father, we lived in the "Treasury", which means "Body" in the inner sanctuary under the throne in the secret place under God's shadow.

> *"He shall hide me in His inner chamber. In the secret place of His sanctuary, He shall hide me, and He shall set me high upon a rock." (Psalm 27:5)*

The Heavenly Mountain was known as "Heaven and earth", and at the top was a hidden garden sanctuary with a great foundation stone[20]. At the entrance was a large hewn stone of which inside was the inherence of peace, the chosen children of God.

> *"His temple was a tall mountain whose summit resembles the throne of God where the eternal King will sit when he descends to visit the earth with goodness. As far as the fragrant tree, not a single human has authority to touch it until the great judgment. And the elect will be presented with its fruit for life." (1 Enoch 25:3-5)*

> *"Listen to Me, you who follow after righteousness. You who seek the Lord; Look to the rock from which you were hewn..." (Isaiah 51:1)*

Under the throne immersed in the light and the shadow of God was the Temple (Rev 21:22), the Holy of Holies (inner sanctuary). It housed the Ark of the Testimony, also called the 'debir', meaning 'word' or 'oracle', it was where God spoke to His anointed servants.[21]

---

[20] Jewish tradition says that on that stone is written the mysteries of God.
[21] Dinah Dye, The Temple Revealed in the Garden, Foundations in Torah Publishing, 2015, p.43

We must remember that we were chosen in Him from the foundation of the world to be holy and blameless (Ephesians 1:4).

Dinah Dye, says,

> "In the Dead Sea Scrolls (4Q418), Adams descendants who will obey are described as 'walking in an eternal plantation'. The main task of this vocation is image bearing reflecting the praises of all creation back to its maker. Those who do so are the royal priesthood, and the Kingdom of Priests."[22]

This is where the King gave out a variation of royal decrees written on a scroll to each member of His body. This is where we received our irrevocable callings (Rom 11:29), before being drawn into a divine council, or another name given is the assemble of the saints. This is also where we were in the royal household of God as a royal priesthood.

> "My frame was not hidden from You, when I was made in secret, and skilfully wrought in the lowest parts of the earth. Your eyes saw my substance, being yet unformed, and in Your book they all were written the days fashioned for me, when as yet there were none of them." (Psalm 139:15-16)

Our frame is our spirit (soul) that was not hidden in the secret place under the shadow of God's wings. We were skilfully "wrought" meaning, made or fashioned in a specified way in the lowest parts of the earth[23]. The lowest parts of the earth is talking about above and the Heavenly Mountain, called "Heaven and Earth" deep in Eden under the throne. An inner sanctuary

---

[22] p.43
[23] "Lowest places of the earth" is used of the unseen world (Psalm 63:9; comp. Psalm 86:13).

that was like a cave deep in the earth. God saw our substance as we had come forth, being yet unformed, not formed in clay, and all our days were fashioned in a book, when as yet there were none of them (until born into the earth, into fallen creation).

In the sanctuary, sat the Ark of the Covenant, of which Enoch called, the House of the Tongues of Fire. A fire that preserved the good righteous seed (souls). The Ark was a mysterious house of existence. It was the place that all children of God, spirit's (souls) lived[24].

> *"Before I formed you in the womb I knew you, before you were born I sanctified you, I ordained you a prophet to the nations." (Jeremiah 1:5)*

Ian Clayton says,

> *"In the beginning YHVH sat as a bench of three in His council and from under the shepherd's rod Jeremiah received the scroll of records for his life. It was from this arena and from this governmental bench that Jeremiah was ordained to bear out his scroll on the face of the earth. In the beginning YHVH provided the source of everything for Jeremiah, when he was released to come to the earth, from within the relationship of YHVH. YHVH sets in place and ordains your walk to fulfil a mandate that you agreed with Him before coming to live in this Adamic form. Your mission and reason for coming to the earth was to fulfil that mandate. YHVH has a plan to unfold for your life, but*

---

[24] Our spirit, comes on a descent and the 'word' (seed) becomes flesh. The womb is a cosmic portal that births multidimensional beings into the matrix. God has the keys to unlock the womb, first from the 'Treasury of Souls', then in to the womb of creation. And then a woman opens her womb and gives birth - 'All that open the womb (matrix) are Mine' (Exodus 34:19).

> *our big problem is that we have amnesia about what the plan was. We get amnesia by the encasing of our spirit man by our physical body and soul, then by retaining our record of the memory of Heaven by overlaying them with the knowledge gleaned and framed by the physical world we live in. So we lose the memory of what we came out of and what we were called to do.*"[25]

> *"Quicken to me after thy loving-kindness, so that I keep the testimony of thy mouth." (Psalm 119:88)*

The Ark of the Covenant, or Ark of the Testimony, held God's Word, on the tablets of stone. Jesus refereed to the word as (seed). This Ark, house, held the Testimonies of "us" for we are called precious stones and a royal priesthood.

> *"You also, as living stones, are being built up a spiritual house, a holy priesthood, to offer up spiritual sacrifices acceptable to God through Jesus Christ." (1 Peter 2:5)*

In the Ark, in the secret garden sanctuary, we were given a scroll of our days, that would give a testimony to God. *"For, 'they overcame him by the blood of the lamb and the word of their testimony."* (Rev 12:11)[26]

Coming out of God into the Ark, House, Temple, secret garden, we met with God and encountered His love and our purpose for our existence. The Ark sits under God's throne, under the mercy seat.

---

[25] Ian Clayton, Realms of the Kingdom, Volume Two, Sons and Thunder Publications, 2016, p.16
[26] Ian Clayton, has a good Chapter, in the book noted, called 'Unlocking your scroll and destiny" (Chapter 1).

The pattern above, is the pattern below[27],

> *"And they shall make an ark of Acacia wood...And you shall overlay its with pure hold, inside and out...And you shall put into the ark the Testimony which I will give you. You shall make a mercy seat of pure gold...And you shall make two cherubim of gold; of hammered work you shall make them at two ends of the mercy seat...And the cherubim shall stretch out their wings above, covering the mercy seat with their wings, and they shall face one another, the faces of the cherubim shall be towards the mercy seat...And there I will met with you, and I will speak with you from above the mercy seat, from between the two cherubim which are on the ark of the testimony" (Exodus 25:10-11)*

The Ark, the House of Fire is like a woman's ovaries, there are two just like two cherubim over the Ark. We came forth from God like a flash of light before the mercy seat, and into the Treasury which is like a womb, of which flows into the garden space[28].

Jesus being born by immaculate conception is a powerful truth reflecting "us" coming out of God, and into the Ark of the Testimony in the Treasury in Heaven[29].

---

[27] They serve at a sanctuary that is a copy and shadow of what is in Heaven. This is why Moses was warned when he was about to build the tabernacle: "See to it that you make everything according to the pattern shown you on the mountain." (Hebrews 8:5)

[28] In darkness we were conceived in Heaven, concluding with our existence out of light. This is also reflected in a woman's body, in the dark conception takes place in the fallopian tubes near the ovaries (Ark), and Science says, in that moment there is a flash of light on the outside of the single cell. This is the portal we enter into the earth and our mother's womb.

[29] "The prophet David danced before the Ark. Now what else should we say the Ark was, but Mary. The Ark bore within it the tablets of the Testament, but Mary

When we are sent from heaven, as a spirit (soul) into our mother's womb at conception it is very much like entering a holy portal to another world. In a later chapter, we will look at the nature and concept of the sending of the soul at conception from a Jewish understanding. But for now, we will reflect on how the Temple (sanctuary) above is very much like a woman's body below on earth.

Above; we came out of God - into the House of Fire; inner sanctuary (Temple) - as a "word" engraved in a precious stone (our spirit/soul fashioned) in the Ark of the Testimony to come to earth to be that testimony revealed. The covenant was made and we were sent, through a portal. We left the garden and were reborn into the earth. As above, so below, as we left the garden above, so we entered the garden portal below. Scripture says, the vagina is like a garden (4:12 Song of Solomon)[30].

Below; the Temple symbolizes the human body, man and woman, but especially the woman's body. The body is a Temple, a house of God, and at conception an embryo is formed (the soul enters) to grow in the womb. The earthly Temple had Pillars which represented a woman's legs. The Porch had no real doors and remained open symbolizing the vulva - the vaginal opening. The double doors at the second entrance to the Holy of Holies related to the hymen - the seal of membrane that only virgins have[31]. The Golden doors symbolizes a betrothed

---

bore the Heir of the same Testament. The former contained in it the Law, the latter the Gospel. The one had the voice of God, the other His Word. The Ark, indeed, was radiant within and without with gold, and Mary shone within and without. The one was adorned with earthly gold, the other with heavenly. (Saint Ambrose 339 AD, Blessed Virgin). - Every Mother's womb is a type of Ark.

[30] Dr. Joseph Dillow says - a locked, or enclosed garden is the image of virginity, and the word 'garden' is a reference to the vagina.

[31] In biblical terms breaking the hymen through sex was symbolic of entering

woman, a bride, waiting for two to become one, then holy only for one.

In the body, the Temple, through the Garden, (the vagina), up into the womb and ovaries, sits the Holy of Holies, and is where the start of conception takes place. As a woman is entered through the hymen, she is betrothed, and becomes a bride. This act represents "us" in heaven as the bride of Christ in the Garden, Temple, Ark in the Treasury under the mercy seat coming forth from God. Can you see how sacred the act of sex is and defiling it is almost like defiling the Holy of Holies in heaven.

From heaven encounters one has learned that the access to the garden is under the throne, and is through a forest through a cave. Caves in the ancient world represented the inner sanctum of a Temple. A woman's "mound" (meaning an embankment) is like a mountain with a forest (pubic hair) of which the entrance is like entering into a cave (vagina) that opens deep into the secret place.

Peter Kreeft in his book, 'Love is Stronger than Death", says,

> *"A mother, then, is essentially a canal (at lest from a biological point of view). Now a birth canal is a door - a magic door, in fact, not merely a door from one part of the world to another, but a door from one whole world to another.... Imagine how you would feel if you discovered such a door in the so-called real world!"*[32]

---

the Eternal Covenant of marriage in blood. Like all biblical covenants they are sealed by the shedding of blood. The Hebrew word for 'covenant', means 'to cut'. There was also a written contract called the Ketubah, under the Huppah (a covering cloud). In Heaven, all of God's chosen entered into a marriage contract of agreements.

[32] Peter Kreeft, Love is Stronger than Death, Ignatius Publishing, 1992, p.60

God showed Abram that there were many descendants in the sky to be born, that is stars (spirit's/elohim) to come down.

> *"Then He brought him outside and said, look now toward heaven, and count the stars if you are able to number them. And he said to him, "So shall your descendants be." (Genesis 15:5)*

As we close this Chapter, we have clearly seen the origin of our existence. In the next chapter, we will look at what the Bible says about the hidden mystery.

CHAPTER 5 - THE HIDDEN MYSTERY

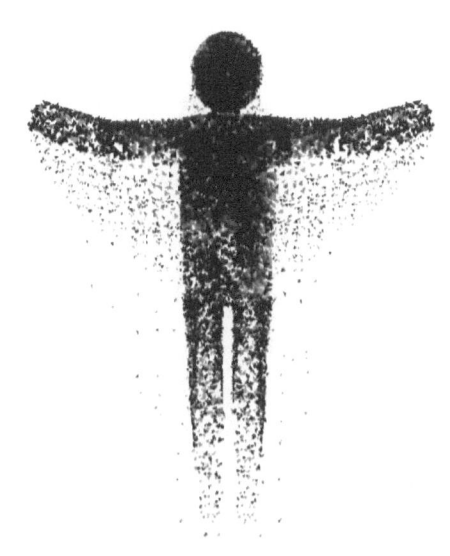

"Mystery Hidden before the Ages; Remember the former things of Old"

Following the truths that were revealed in the last Chapter, that we existed in heaven. In this Chapter, we will lay a foundation using Scriptures that talk about the "Hidden Mystery".

> *"But we speak the wisdom of God in a mystery, the hidden wisdom which God ordained before the ages for our glory." (1 Corinthians 2:7)*

Before we look into this mystery that was hidden, yes, there was "something hidden" that was ordained before the ages for our glory; I will quickly recap what we have covered in Chapter Two.

* God is eternal, and He is the highest Elohim, before creation, He created the angels (lower elohim), and also brought forth the light of the world, the eternal Son (Jesus) to light up the visible creation under Him, and the angels shouted for joy and sang in wonder. Out of God, the Trinity decreed, and "We" were brought forth from His light, in His light, the light of men (and woman) (John 1:3) in to an eternal covenant (Heb 13:20). We were brought forth created as "spirits of just men" and pre-existed in heaven. We were created a little lower than the angels, different from them, but also part of the royal house-hold, the family of God.

We are also a type of elohim; Scripture says, "We were chosen in Him (Christ) from the foundation of the world." We existed before the foundation of the world, and this is attested to in the Scriptures, and in many other ancient texts. We were also part of a divine council before the foundation of the world.

So let us now look at the verse in 1 Corinthians 2:7 - *"But we speak the wisdom of God in a mystery, the hidden wisdom which God ordained before the ages for our glory."*

We are told that God is revealing in His word to us that He in His wisdom, hid a mystery, not just secret knowledge, but a real mystery, which was ordained before the ages for our glory. It is the mystery of the Kingdom, a people chosen to be image bearers of God. He chose us in Him before the foundation of the world (Eph 1:4). As sons of God, we were sent into the world (now fallen) to live in a flesh body, of which we see dimly to pass through the earth, over-coming and transforming in humility and in the art of love to go from glory to glory to be revealed and freed as the glorious sons of God (Rom 8:19). We will also be resurrected, and be exalted above the angels, and also judge them. But my point is - "WE" existed in heaven first, we are the glorious hidden mystery betrothed to Christ!!!! In a flash of created light from God we were separated and betrothed to Him[33].

* We were chosen in Him before the foundation of the world (Eph 1:4)

* We were a hidden mystery ordained for glory (1 Cor 2:7)

---

[33] Abraham was caught up and shown a vision; "And He said to me, 'These upon the left side are the multitude of former generations, and those to come after you. These for judgment and order; these for vengeance and destruction at the end of the world. But those on the right of the picture are the people chosen for Me, separate from the peoples of Azazel. These are those which I have prepared to be born through you and to be called My people." (The Apocalypse of Abraham, 70 - 150 AD) - "For You were slain, And redeemed us to God by Your blood "Out" of every tribe and tongue and people and nation." (Rev 5:9) - And, "Then the King will say to those on His right hand, you blessed of My Father, inherit the Kingdom prepared for you from the foundation of the world." (Matt 25:34)

- We sat in a divine council, the assemble of the saints (Psalm 89)

- We are the mystery of the Kingdom (Parables)

- The Kingdom was prepared for us before the foundation of the world (Matt 25:31-36)

- Our names were written in the Book of Life before the foundation of the world (Rev 13:8)

- Our days to be lived on earth, were fashioned and written in a scroll book. (Psalm 139:16)

- We were given our irrevocable callings (Rom 11:29)

- Eternity has also been the "nature of our 'essence' - Home. Written upon our hearts. (Ecc 3:11)

- The New Jerusalem existed in Heaven before the ages, and the Apostles names are written into the walls of it (Rev 21:14)

- The Church was in Eden, The Church of God, maybe even the spirits of just men, Church of the first born pointed to in (Heb 12:23)

- The Spirit Himself bears witness with our spirit that we are the children of God (Rom 8:16)

- Like John who was sent into the world to bear the witness of the light (John 1:6), so are we sent into the world (John 17:18) - predestined into it (Rom 8:30)

- Having made known to us the mystery of his will, according to His good pleasure which He purposed in Himself. (Eph 1:9).

The Shepherd of Hermas, an early Christian work that many read, says, of the pre-existent Church, "She was created before all things, for her sake was the world framed (2:41)".

> *"Lord, You have been our dwelling place in all ages, before the mountains were brought forth, Or ever You had formed the earth and the world, Even from everlasting to everlasting You are God." (Psalm 90:1-2)*

> *"He who dwells in the secret place of the Most High, shall abide under the shadow of the almighty. I will say of the Lord, He is my refuge and my fortress, My God, in him I will trust." (Psalm 91:1-2)*

> *"Where is the way to the dwelling of light?" (Job 38:20)*

Adam and all generations were created and lived in God before the foundation of the world. They lived in his light, in His dwelling place, the secret place, this fortress in Paradise at the side of the North. Paradise is different to the "Garden" that is in Paradise (Eden). We lived in what the Jews call the Gulf, a Treasury of Souls. What is fascinating to note is the word "Guf or Gulf" means "Body" and the word "Treasury" means more than a treasure box, it is a secret place in the light of God among the stones of fire.

The word "North" also has some revealing revelation, it can mean, hidden, covered over, to hoard, reserved, favoured, protected, hide one self, keep secret, secret place, to hid, store treasure, laid up. Scripture tells us that the congregation or assemble exists in the North, "I will sit also upon the mount of the **congregation**, in the sides of the **north**" (Isa 14:13). This stored treasure that is in the congregation is 'us', we are the mystery.

One writer says,

> "This reason is why the Hebrew term for the 'North' alludes to a mystical location, a hidden or secret place. Understanding these connections one can then make sense of the underlying truth conjoining all of these seemingly disjointed stories. צָפוֹן tsâphôwn, tsaw-fone'; or צָפֹן tsâphôn; from H6845; properly, hidden, i.e., dark; used only of the north as a quarter (gloomy and unknown): — north (-ern, side, -ward, wind). north (of direction), northward north northward צָפַן tsâphan, tsaw-fan'; a primitive root; to hide (by covering over); by implication, to hoard or reserve; figuratively to deny; specifically (favorably) to protect, (unfavorably) to lurk: — esteem, hide (hidden one, self), lay up, lurk (be set) privily, (keep) secret(-ly, place).
>
> To hide, treasure, treasure or store up (Qal) to hide, treasure, treasure up to lie hidden, lurk (Niphal) to be hidden, be stored up (Hiphil) to hide, hide from discovery The feminine noun צָפוֹן tsâphôwn (North) comes from the verb form and primitive root of tsâphan meaning hidden, hoarded, reserved, protected, is steamed, laid up, treasured, stored up, and or secret place. Does not such connotation add to the mystery?"[34]

In this secret place we existed when we were created and brought forth from the light of God before the foundation of the world.

---

[34] Zen Garcia, Paradise: Sides of the North and the Mount of Congregation, Lulu.com Publishers, 2017.

Jesus as the head, and us in Him, His body - for we are the body of Christ, we were in the Treasury, Guf (body). If we merge them together, we have Jesus's body (two become one).

> *"If one part suffers, every part suffers with it; if one part is honoured, every part rejoices with it. Now you are the body of Christ, and each of you is a member of it. And in the church of God..." (1 Corinthians 12:27).*

Christ loves His Church, like a husband should love his wife - and they become one flesh. That is what marriage represents. We were chosen in Christ before the foundation of the world, to be His body, to be one flesh with Him in perfect intimacy, as His bride.

The problem is, we "see" dimly so we don't remember (1 Cor 13:12). When we are sent, and from Jewish tradition, our memory is set to forget the former things (world above). We are then born into the earth with little knowledge, grasping for God's existence, until we are born again to remember 'Who" we really are.

We are born into a fallen world, a dark world, and we do not see as we should.

> *"Remember the former things of old, For I am God, and there is none like Me; declaring the end from the beginning, and from ancient times things that are not yet done." (Isaiah 46:9-10)*

> *"Shall Your wonder be known in the dark? And Your righteousness in the land of forgetfulness? But to You I have cried out, O Lord, and in the morning my prayer comes before you." (Psalm 88:12-13)*

The earth is a dark place that we see dimly, Jesus even said, that He came into the world to shine the light, but the darkness did not comprehend it, or receive it. (John 1:5:11)

When we are "sent" into the earth as a soul (spirit) to enter into our formed flesh bodies at conception, we leave heaven through the dwelling of the light portal, and enter into the gates of death (portal into the dark fallen world), through the doors, into the world of the shadow of death. The world is a shadow of heaven.

> *"Have the gates of death been revealed to you? Or have you seen the doors of the shadow of death? Have you comprehended the breadth of the earth? Tell Me, if you know all this. Where is the way to the dwelling of light? And darkness, where is its place. That you may take it to its territory, that you may know the paths to its home?" (Job 38:17-20)*

"For we were born yesterday, and know nothing, our days on earth are like a shadow." (Job 8:9)

Psalm 23:1-3 depicts the realms of heaven and earth, the light and the shadow,

> *"The Lord is my shepherd; I shall not want. He makes me lie down in green pastures, He leads me beside the still waters, He restores my soul, He leads me in paths of righteousness for His name's sake" (Psalm 23:1-3)*

Verse 1-3 are talking about being in Eden, but from verse 4 it is talking about living in the shadow of death in the earth.

"Yea, though I walk through the valley of the shadow of death, I will fear no evil, for You are with me. Your staff and Your rod, they comfort me." (Psalm 23:4)

"For I consider that the sufferings of this present time are not worthy to be compared with the glory which shall be revealed in us. For the earnest expectation of the creation eagerly waits for the revealing of the sons of God." (Romans 8:18-19)

Though we walk through a dark world, God promises us that He will never leave us or forsake us, and nothing can separate us from His love (Rom 9:39). We are the manifesting, revealing, transforming mystery in the earth.

CHAPTER 6 - THE ETERNAL EDEN CHURCH

> *"But you have come to Mount Zion and to the city of the living God, the heavenly Jerusalem, to an innumerable company of angels, to the general assembly and church of the first born who are registered in heaven to God the judge of all, to the spirits of just men made perfect." (Hebrews 12:22-23)*

The Church has existed in Eden from the very beginning at the top of Mount Zion. We are told of three groups that exist there, the angels, the general assembly, and the Church of the first born who are registered in heaven, to the spirits of just men made perfect. I would say,' we are all members of the Church'[35], but there are a few writers who believe there is, the general assembly (the assembly of the saints), and then the Church of the first born, which is an ancient order that was for the first-born patriarchs in Israel. They say that heaven has ancient orders (like fraternities) that some are a part of, and that there is even an order called the "Order of the Father".

1 Enoch 70:4 says, "He saw the fathers of the righteous who from the beginning dwelt in that place."

Even Jesus was a part of an ancient order, Psalm 110:4,

> *"The Lord has sworn, and will not relent, You are a priest forever according to the order of Melchizedek." (Psalm 110:4)*

Zen Garcia says of these ancient orders,

> *"The earliest priesthood mentioned in the Bible, is alluded to as the order of Melchizedek. Melchizedek*

---

[35] That is all those that were chosen in Christ from the foundation of the world.

meaning 'king of righteousness.' In Psalms 110, Yahushua Christ is spoken of as holding position in this ancient order. "The Lord hath sworn, and will not repent, thou art a priest for ever after the order of Melchizedek." While this ancient group remains ambiguous and little defined within the canonical materials, we discover in the extra biblical texts much information which when examined, elaborates in great detail on the structure, association, and the membership of certain patriarchs to this time worn organization.

Many scholars having been interested in this concept and likewise because so many of you have asked me to make available in print for public consideration, The Book of the Order is said to have been written by Elijah the prophet. I decided to release this title. An extract from the Kitab-Al Magalli included within this manuscript, verifies scripturally that Adam in paradise before his fall, was ordained by God and trained by His angels to assume in what is cited as the church of Eden, the role of priest, king, and prophet."[36]

A number of early Church Fathers also recognized that the Church existed from eternity,

"And the books and apostles declare that the church is not the present, but is from the beginning. For she was spiritual" (Second Clement, 150 AD).

"He said, it is the church. And I said to him, Why is she an old woman? He replied, because she was created first of all. On

---

[36] https://sacredwordpublishing.com/products/book-of-the-order-of-the-ancients

this account she is old. And the world was made for her sake." (Hermas, 150 AD).

"For the church has been planted as a garden in this world" (Irenaeus, 180 AD).

"The earthly church is the image of the heavenly" (Clement of Alexandria, 195 AD).

"The peace of God is sent out from heaven where the church is, the typified ark" (Tertullian, 197 AD).

"His church is that very stone in Daniel, cut out of the mountain, which was to smite and crush the image of secular kingdoms." (Tertullian, 207 AD).

"We cling to the standard of the heavenly church of Jesus Christ according to the succession of the apostles." (Origen, 225 AD).

"The church resembles Paradise. She includes within her walls fruit bearing trees. But that which does not bring forth good fruit is cut off. These trees she waters with the four rivers - that is, with the four gospels with which, by heavenly outpouring, she bestows the grace of saving baptism." (Cyprian, 250 AD).

"According to the Song of Song, the church is a garden enclosed and a fountain sealed - a Paradise with the fruit of apples." (Firmilian, 256 AD).

The Church Father Clement of Alexandra wrote in Padagogeis, "God knew us before the foundation of the world, and chose us for our faithfulness even at that time. Now we have become babes to fulfil the plan of God." (195 AD).

1 Enoch 62;7-8 - describes the Son of Man together with the congregation of the Elect before their sowing in the earth.

The Qumran Hymn Scroll, which speaks of a pre-existent community as a "Mystery", a tree fed from a secret spring" (1 QH 8;4-11).

In the Dead Sea Scrolls (4 Q 418), Adam's descendants, 'who will obey are described as "walking in an eternal plantation."

The early Christian Odes of Solomon (70-100 AD) also describes the pre-existence church as a community of 'fruit bearing trees", who's crown is self-grown, and who roots are from a immortal land watered by a river of gladness (Ode 11).

The Church, the true people of God find their existence in eternity. The elect that where in Christ before the foundation of the world were the first Church in Eden. We were hidden in Him, like in an Ark, fortress, wall of glory, all around us. We were His body, in His temple, we are His building (1 Cor 3:9) among the stones of fire. We were hidden in Him, on the Rock of Zion, the foundation stone.

> *"Let a man consider us, as servants of Christ and the stewards of the mysteries of God." (1 Corinthians 4:1)*

CHAPTER 7 - THE EVIDENCE SPEAKS

In this Chapter, we will document extensively references that point to "who" we are, and where we came from and once lived, that being - our first estate in heaven. Many think this idea is kind of from a fringe group, or a belief one or two Church Fathers held, but this is not the case.

The references are under sub-headings and they give us great insights into what was believed. The sub-headings are as follows,

In the Beginning, - Jewish Theology, - The Book of Enoch, - The Mystery, - Jewish Texts, - Early Church Fathers, - Jewish Thoughts on Conception, - Mystics, -Scriptures of the Spirit/Soul in Heaven, - Even Islam,

In the Beginning!

(1) In the beginning was the Word, and the Word was with God, and the Word was God. He was in the beginning with God. All things were made through Him and without Him nothing was made that was made. In Him was life, and the life was the light of men." (John 1:3) - God the Word was eternal, and in Him, from His light, (created light), He brought forth the light of men in eternity.

(2) In the beginning God planted a Cosmic Tree, and all spirit's (souls) blossomed from it, flying forth in joy. All things emanate from its light. The Tree is the Life of God.[37]

---

[37] Interesting to note, Scripture calls us precious stones, and in, 'The Epic of Gilgamesh', it speaks of a tree in paradise that bears precious gems (tablet 9)

From this Tree blossomed forth all spirit's (souls) that will ever be, as it is said, "I am like a Cypress Tree in bloom, your fruit issues forth from Me." (Hos 14:9) And from the root of the Tree sprouts all the ones whose names are inscribed there.

"And He has written eternity on their hearts." (Ecclesiastes 3:11). The names are written in the root of Life, their birth of existence, and eternity, their foundation, home, source of life, is written in their spirit's heart.

(3) "We were chosen in Christ before the foundation of the world...." (Ephesians 1:4)

(4) "Having made known to us the mystery of His will, according to His good pleasure which He purposed in Himself." (Ephesians 1:9).

What is this mystery? the mystery of the Kingdom? the mystery that was in Him from the foundation of the world? It is those who are in Christ in the Treasury of light to come forth.

(5) "Before I formed you in the womb I knew you, before you were born, I set you apart; I appointed you as a prophet to the nations." (Jeremiah 1:5)

(6) Jesus said, "I have given them Your word, and the world has hated them because they are not of the world, just as I am not of the world. I do not pray that you should take them out of the world, but that You should keep them from the evil one. They are not of the world, just as I am not of the world. Sanctify them by Your truth. Your word is truth. <u>As You sent Me</u>

<u>into the world, I also have sent them into the world.</u>... For You have sent Me and have loved them as You have loved me.... For You loved Me before the foundation of the world." (John 17:14-18,23,24)

(7) The mystery unfolding and transforming is "Us" awakening to who "We" truly are. We see in part on the earth, in a mirror dimly of who we truly reflected in the mirror, that being the full image of God in His light and Glory in eternity. (1 Cor 13:12). We are not an accident, but a child of God, sent with a purpose. we see dimly because we have stepped into a fallen world, fallen short of glory of God.

Jewish Theology!

(8) From the Tree of Life; spirit's (souls) drop off and end up in the "Treasury of Souls" (another name used Guf) under the Throne.

(9) Heaven Testimony; has revealed a place of flickering lights, like candles, little souls, with cries of "send me, send me" for your glory".

(10) The Talmud states, 'The Son of David will come before all the souls in the Guf have been disposed of." Another Talmud sage says, "The Messiah will only come when all the souls destined to inhabit bodies have been exhausted."[38]

---

[38] Many of the Jewish references can be found in the book by 'Howard, Schwartz, *Tree of Souls; The Mythology of Judaism,* Oxford University Press, 2004'.

(11) In Jewish thought God takes a soul out of the Treasury, and before sending it touches it on his upper lip so that it forgets the joys of heaven, so that it can adapt to the world into which they are born. Just before they are sent an angel of conception takes the soul down and infuses it into the embryo with the breath of God's spirit in the womb on earth.

(12) With Adam, his spirit (soul) was sent down breathed in to his body by God and his spirit shone through him and around him with light like a garment.

(13) The Jews believe - That all spirit's that would ever live, were brought into existence before the foundation of the world. This is a general belief by most Rabbis. Jewish Scholar Simcha Paull Raphael in his book 'Jewish views of the Afterlife', says, the idea of the soul/spirit coming into existence for the first time at conception is Aristotle thinking (Greek).[39]

The Book of Enoch!

(14) 1 Enoch 62:7-8 - describes the Son of Man together with the congregation of the Elect before their sowing in the earth.

(15) "All souls are prepared for eternity, before the composition of the earth." (2 Enoch 23)

---

[39] Simcha Paull Raphael, Jewish Views of the Afterlife, Roman & Littefield, 2019

(16)   1 Enoch 70:4 says, "He saw the fathers of the righteous who from the beginning dwelt in that place."

(17)   "And I swear to you, that there has been no man in his mother's womb, but that already before, even to each one there is a place prepared for repose of the soul, and a measure fixed how much it is intended that a man be tried in this world. Yea children, deceive not yourselves, for there has been previously prepared a place for every soul of man." (2 Enoch 49:3)

(18)   In 3 Enoch (Hebrew Enoch), Rabbi Ishmael, the recipient of the vision, is shown the spirits of the righteous who are yet to be born (3 Enoch 43:1)

The Mystery!

(19)   The Qumran Hymn Scroll, which speaks of a pre-existent community as a "Mystery", a tree fed from a secret spring (1 QH 8;4-11).

(20)   In the Dead Sea Scrolls (4Q 418), Adam's descendants 'who will obey are described as "walking in an eternal plantation."

(21)   The early Christian Odes of Solomon (70-100 AD) also describes the pre-existence church as a community of "fruit bearing trees", who's crown is self-grown, and who roots are from a immortal land watered by a river of gladness (Ode 11)

THE EVIDENCE SPEAKS

(22) The Shepherd of Hermas, an early text Christian's read, says, 'of the pre-existent Church, "She was created before all things, for her sake was the world framed (2:41)."

(23) Another ancient text says, "For this cause have I chosen you verily from the beginning through the First Mystery. I have taken from the Treasury of Light, according to the command of the First Mystery. These I cast into womb of your mothers. For which cause I have said unto you indeed from the beginning that you are not of the world. But the power that is in you is from Me, your souls belong to the height." (Pistis Sophia)

Jewish Texts!

(24) The Syiac Apocalypse of Burach says, "The storehouse in which the foreordained number of souls is kept shall be opened and the souls shall go forth; and the many shall appear at once, as a host with one mind."

(25) 1st Century – Of the pre-existence of Moses, mention is made in Assumption of Moses (1:14): "He designed me and prepared me before the foundation of the world that I should be the mediator of the Covenant."

(26) - According to Josephus, the Essenes affirmed the pre-existence of souls.

(27) - "Book of Jubilees says, "On the first day of creation, God made, "All of the spirits of His creatures which

minister before Him, several angelic beings, and all of the spirits of His creatures that are in Heaven and earth." (2 Cen C.E)

(28)   4 Ezra - "Those in heaven ask when will they be free from the storehouse of souls and are told only after all those like themselves had experience mortality (earth life) for the times and season were numbered."

(29)   The Apocalypse of Abraham gives this description of a Heavenly council,

And I said: "Primeval One, Strong One, what is this picture of the creature?" And he said to me: "This is my will in relation to that which has a being in the Council, and it became pleasing before me, and then afterwards I commanded them to be through my word. *And it came to pass that as many as I had authorized to exist, before portrayed in this picture, and had stood before me precreated, —as many as you have seen,"*

And I said: "Ruler, Strong One, Thou Who Wast Before the World, who are the multitude in this picture, on the right hand and on the left?"

And He said to me: *"These upon the left side are the multitude of former generations, and those to come after you. These for judgment and order; these for vengeance and destruction at the end of the world. But those on the right side of the picture are the people chosen for me, separate from the peoples of Azazel. These are those which I have prepared to be born through you and to be called my people."* (Abraham 22).

Early Church Fathers!

(30) The Church Father Clement of Rome 95 AD, a companion of Paul said, quoting Peter, "Last of all, He made man whose real nature is older, however for who's sake all this was created."

(31) The Church Father Clement of Alexandra wrote in Padagogeis, "God knew us before the foundation of the world, and chose us for our faithfulness even at that time. Now we have become babes to fulfil the plan of God."

(32) Church Father Justin Martyr (160 AD) "Whenever a soul must cease to exist, the spirit is removed from it, and there is no more soul. Rather, it goes back to the place from where it was taken."

(33) - Philip Schaff, History of the Christian Church; mentions others as holding views similar to Origen: Even Gregory of Nyssa, although, like Nemesius and Cyril of Alexandria, he supposed the soul to be created before the body.[40]

(34) Early Church Father Lactantius said, the soul comes directly from God, while the body is derived from physical material. A body may be produced from a body, since something is contributed from both, father and mother, but a soul cannot be produced from souls, souls belong entirely to God along.[41]

---

[40] Phillip Schaff, History of the Christian Church (Volumes 1-8) e.book version.
[41] Many of the Church Fathers quotes in - 'David Bercot, A Dictionary of Early Christian Beliefs, Hendrickson Publishers, 1998'.

(35) Early Church Father Cyprian said, For since we possess the body from the earth and the spirit from heaven, we ourselves are both earth and heaven; and in both, that is both in body and spirit.[42]

(36) The Church Father Augustine held that the soul/spirit was in Heaven before it came to earth.

Jewish Thoughts on Conception!

(37) "IX. (1) I will now proceed to explain the formation of the fœtus which God created when man approaches his wife. God indicates it to the angel appointed over conception, whose name is Lailah. God says, 'Know that this night a woman will conceive. Take this sperm, place it in thy hand, and break it on the threshing-floor into three hundred and sixty-five particles.' He does so. He then takes the sperm in his hand, brings it to God, and says, 'O Lord of the world, I have done as Thou hast commanded me, and now decree what is to become of it.' God then decrees that it will be either strong or weak, male or female, rich or poor, beautiful or ugly, long or short.

God then makes a sign to the angel appointed over spirits, and says, 'Bring me a certain spirit which is hidden in the Garden of Eden, whose name is So-and-so, and whose form is So-and-so.' This applies to all the spirits which are destined to be created, for

---

[42] Gregg Allison, Historical Theology, An Introduction to Christian Doctrine, Zondervan, 2011, p. 326.

from the very moment when the world was created all (these spirits) were prepared for men, as it is said, 'What has already been has been called by name.' The angel brings the (said) spirit, which, when it comes before God, bows down and prostrates itself before Him.

At that moment God says to the spirit, 'Enter thou this sperm.' The spirit then opens its mouth, and says, 'O Lord of the universe, I am satisfied with the world in which I have lived from the day on which Thou didst create me; if it please Thee, do not suffer me to enter this impure being, for I am holy and pure.' God replies, 'The world which I will cause thee to enter is better than the world in which thou hast lived (better than just sitting in the treasury); and when I created thee, I created thee only for this purpose.'

God then causes it to enter this new being against its will. The angel then returns and causes it to enter the womb of its mother. Two angels are prepared to watch the embryo (during pregnancy). A light shines upon the head of the child, by which it sees from one end of the world to the other.

In the morning the angel takes it, carries it into the Garden of Eden and shows it the righteous men who sit there in glory with crowns on their heads. The angel then says to the soul, 'My child, dost thou know who these are?' 'No,' it replies. The angel then says, 'These people whom thou seest here were formed like thee in the womb of their mother. They went forth into the world and observed God's statutes, therefore they became worthy of this bliss. Know also that thou wilt at the end of thy days depart from the world. and if thou wilt be thought worthy to hearken unto the Law and the Commandments then thou wilt be likewise worthy of sitting with these in the place where I showed thee.'

In the evening he carries it into Gehinnom, and shows it the sinners, whom the wicked angels beat with fiery staves. They cry 'Woe, woe!' but no mercy is shown them. The angel then says to the soul, 'Dost thou know, my child, who these are that burn?' 'No,' it replies. The angel answers, 'These were of the same mean origin as thou art. They went forth to the world and did not observe the commandments and judgments of God. Therefore, they have come to this place of punishment. Know also, child, that thou must ultimately quit this world.'

The angel walks about with it from morning until evening, and shows it every place which it is destined to tread, and the place where it will be buried. After this he shows it the world of the good and the world of the wicked, and in the evening, he places it back again in the womb of its mother. God then encloses it within folded doors, as it is said, 'And He shut in the sea with doors, until it burst forth from the womb and became free.' It is further said, 'I will lay My words in thy mouth, and I will protect thee in the shadow of My hand.' God then said, 'Thus far shalt thou go, and no further;' and He sustains the child in the womb of its mother for nine months.

At the end of that time the same angel comes and says to it, 'Come forth, for the time has come for thee to go forth into the world.' It replies, 'Have I not already told God that I am satisfied to remain in the place where I was accustomed to dwell? And He replied, "The place I will cause thee to enter is better than that world from which thou hast come." Now that it pleases me to remain here, why dost thou wish to remove me hence?' The angel replies, 'Thou must know that thou wast formed in the womb of thy mother against thy will, and now know that against thy will thou wilt be born, and wilt come forth into the world.' He then immediately strikes it, extinguishes the light, and brings it forth against its will. It then forgets whatever it had seen. As soon as it comes forth unto the world, it cries.

And why does it cry? Because of the world it has left behind. For at that moment seven new worlds are awaiting it. In the first world it is like unto a king after whose welfare all people ask; all desire to see it and embrace it, and kiss it, because it is in the first year. In the second world it is like unto a swine which wallows in mire; a child does the same until it reaches two years. In the third world it is like unto a kid that skips and gambols about on the meadows. Thus, a child skips about here and there until it is five years of age. In the fourth world it is like unto a horse which strides along haughtily.

In the same way does a child walk along proud of his youth until he is eighteen years old. In the fifth world he is like unto an ass upon whose shoulders burdens are placed. In the same manner burdens are heaped upon man's shoulders; he is given a wife by whom he begets children. He must wander to and fro in order to obtain food for them until he is about forty years old. In the sixth stage he is like unto a dog, insolent and wandering about in all places for food: stealing and robbing in one place and enjoying it in another. In the seventh stage he is like unto an ape, whose appearance is changed in every respect. All the household curse him and desire his death. Even the young children make fun of him, and even the smallest bird wakes him from his sleep.

Finally, the time arrives for him to quit this world. When that time arrives the same angel comes beside him and says to him, What is thy name?' To which he replies 'So-and-so, and Why dost thou come to me to-day?' 'To take thee away from this world.' When he hears this, he weeps, and his voice reaches from one end of the world to the other, but no creature hears his voice except the cock. 'Have I not already told thee,' he says, 'not to bring me forth from the world in which I have lived?' But the angel replies, 'Have I not already told thee that against thy will thou wast created, against thy will thou wast born, against thy will thou livest, and against thy will thou shalt die, also against thy will thou art bound to render account and reckoning before Him who said, and the world was made?'

Behold, these are the four Divine hosts which God showed to Elijah the prophet, as it is said, 'And He said, Go out and stand upon the mountain before God.' God then said to Elijah, 'Behold, these are the four worlds through which man must pass. The great and strong wind is this world. After the wind comes the earthquake, *i.e.*, after this world comes death, which causes the whole body of man to quake. After the earthquake comes the fire, *i.e.*, after death there follows the judgment of Gehinnom, which is fire, and after the judgment of Gehinnom there follows a voice, as it is said, 'A still, soft voice,' which is the voice of the last judgment. After this follows the judgment of the spirits that flit about in the air, and no one is left except God, as it is said, 'God alone shall be exalted on that day.' All this is included in the words of holy tradition spoken by David, king of Israel, who said, 'I was made in secret, I was formed in the nethermost parts of the earth." (Legends of the Jews, Lious Ginzberg).[43]

(38) Renowned seventeenth century Rabbi Menasseh Ben Israel held that human souls existed before embodiment, not as an idea in the mind of God, but as entities with whom He actually consulted before creation.

Mystics!

(39) The Mystic Julian Norwitch said –

"I saw that God never began to love mankind. For, just as humanity is bound for eternal bliss in order to satisfy the joy that God prepared for his creation, so mankind has been known and loved from all eternity in the providence of God. For with the eternal assent and agreement of the whole Trinity, the Second Person willed to become the ground and head of this beautiful human nature. We all came from him; we are all comprised in him and to him we are destined to go in order to find our heaven and everlasting joy.

---

[43] Louis Ginzberg, The Legends of the Jews, Four Volumes, Lulu.com, 2018

All this was achieved in the providential purpose of the blessed Trinity from before the beginning of time.

For he loved us before he made us and, after we had been created, we loved him. And this is a love which has been created by the essential goodness of the Holy Spirit. This love is powerful by virtue of the Power of the Father, wise by virtue of the Wisdom of the Son. Man's soul is created by God and united to him in the same instant.

And so, I understood that man's soul was created from nothing, or rather, it has been made but not out of anything created. Thus, when God created man's body, he took clay from the earth, which is a substance composed of many physical elements. And from all this he made man's body.

But he didn't take anything at all when he made man's soul: he just created it. And in this way, created nature was duly united to its Maker, who is essentially uncreated Nature: that is, God. And that is why there neither can nor should be anything at all between God and a man's soul.

Man's soul is preserved whole and entire in God's eternal love, as the revelations show. In this endless love we are guided and preserved by God and will never be lost. For it is his will that we realise that our soul is alive and that this life, through his goodness and grace, will continue in heaven forever, loving, thanking and praising him. And just as we shall be in eternity, in exactly the same way we were treasured and hidden in God, known and loved by him from before the beginning of time. That is why he wants us to know that the noblest thing he ever created is mankind."[44]

Scriptures of the Spirit/Soul in Heaven!

(40)   Scripture points to pre-existence; Father God created all spirits in eternity, because He is our Father - "Further, we have had human fathers who corrected us, and we paid them respect. Shall we not much more readily be in subjection to the Father of spirits and live?" (Heb 12:9).

* God the judge of all, to the spirits of just men made perfect." (Heb 12:23)
* Therefore, since we are the offspring of God..." (Acts 17:29)
* Thus says the Lord, who stretches out the heavens, lays the foundation of the earth, and forms the spirit of man within him." (Zac 12:1)
* And the Lord God formed man of the dust of the ground, and breathed into his nostrils the breath (spirit) of life, and man became a living being." (Gen 2:7)
* Then the dust will return to the earth as it was. And the spirit will return to God who gave it." (Ecc 12:7)
* Who knows the spirit of the sons of men, which goes upward..." (Ecc 3:21) - back to where it came.

---

[44] https://zoepopper.wordpress.com/2018/10/30/julian-of-norwich-nothing-between-god-and-the-soul/

(41) "In Him having been predestined according to the purpose of Him, who works all things according to the counsel of His will" (Eph 1:4)

Even Islam!

(42)   In Islam, all souls are believed to have been created in adult form (before earthly life) at the same time God created the father of mankind, Adam[45]. The Quran recounts the story of when the descendants of Adam were brought forth before God to testify that God alone is the Lord of creation and therefore, only he is worthy of worship so that on the Day of Judgement, people could not make the excuse that they only worshipped others because they were following the ways of their ancestors.

It is kind of hard to believe that some think the doctrine of the pre-existence of the soul is just some off shoot heresy. In this Chapter, I have documented from all groups, from early times that this belief was a solid reality.

---

[45] https://www.islamicity.org/7887/seven-stages-of-life-in-islam/

CHAPTER 8 - COUNCIL OF RIGHTEOUS SOULS

When God said, "Let us make man", in our image and likeness, He was not having an agreement between the Trinity. God (one of the members of the Trinity) was asking in His council, speaking to lower elohim; if they agreed to it (in a council of discussions). That is, should we create "man", a man figure, unique, but like a member of the "house-hold" of Elohim (there are many types of Elohim). This might sound strange to many, but this is what many Scholars believe this text is saying grammar wise.[46]

The word "elohim" is a term given to "spiritual beings", so now let's take this knowledge to the divine councils.

In the divine council in heaven, it says in the Book of Job,[47]

> *"The sons of God came to present themselves before Yahweh" (Job 1:6,2;1)*

Psalm 29: 1–2 summons these same gods to do homage before the Lord, to bow down before Him and praise His name, while Psalm 97:7 likewise bids all the gods to bow down before God. Psalm 103:20–21 is an invocation directed to the celestial assembly, and Psalm 148:2 commands the angels of the Lord, all those who constitute His host, to praise Him. Psalm 97:9 records that God is supreme over all the gods; Psalm 96:4 states that God is to be feared over all the gods; and Psalm 95:3 attests that God is a great king over all the gods.

Then we have Psalm 89:3-8, and Psalm 82:1-2,6-7,

> *"I have made a covenant with My chosen, I have sworn to My servant David, Your seed I will establish forever, And build up your throne to all generations. And the*

---

[46] Biblical Scholar Micheal Heiser.
[47] In Ezekiel 28:2, it speaks of the 'seat of the gods', these are the thrones of the divine council.

heavens will praise Your wonders, O Lord; Your faithfulness also in the assembly of the saints. For who in the heavens can be compared to the Lord? Who among the sons of the mighty can be likened to the Lord? God is greatly to be feared in the assembly of the saints, And to be held in reverence by all those around Him, O Lord of hosts." (Psalm 89:3-8)

"God's stands in the congregation of the mighty. He judges among the gods (elohim) How long will you judge unjustly and show partiality to the wicked...I said, "You are gods, And all of you are children of the Most High, but you shall die like men, and fall like one of the princes." (Psalm 82:1-2,6-7).

This is where it gets interesting, there is a heavenly council, the angels are there (Job 1:6,2:1), then in Psalm 89:3-9, an assembly of the saints, or holy ones are seen in the council (assembly), and then in Psalm 82:1-2, 6-7, we have the term, "I said, you are gods.". This is also the verse Jesus spoke to the Jewish Leaders on, and said to them, 'Is it not written in your law, 'I said, you are gods'. "If he called them gods, to whom the Scriptures cannot be broken..." (John 10:34-35). As one of my friends says, this is the one verse if you address it, you will get your head chopped off. It is a difficult passage, and people many times don't know what they are allowed to conclude.

The verse "I said, "You are gods, and all of you are children of the Most High, but you shall die like men, and fall like one of the princes." in Psalm 82, is an interesting statement. Was He talking just to angels or to both angels and spirit's (souls) elohim (spiritual beings)[48]. That souls would fall one day, and they would be in bodies and die like men (mortals), like also a prince

---

[48] Angels dont seem to be called children of the Most High or men, so is this a title for spirits of men? But angels are called sons of Heaven.

fell above and will die, a spiritual death (Lucifer). I don't know the answer, I'm just putting it out there!? Did some souls rebel in heaven as well as angels?[49]

Rabbi Syliva Rothschild says of Psalm 82,

> *"Just as in the garden of Eden, the Bible is alluding to us having once been immortal and god like beings, who lost this status through an act of not trusting God."*[50]

In John 10:34-35, Jesus is not saying that he is allowed to call himself the Son of God because every other Jew could. This would undermine Jesus' claim to deity, and being one with the Father. Jesus is saying, 'He is one with the Father the highest Elohim', and this irritates the Jews, but Jesus reminds them that they should know this as they were in the divine council once upon a time as gods.[51]

It might surprise many that the early Church Fathers didn't (on the whole) have a problem with this verse. In a later chapter, we will quote from many of them, but for now we will look at two Theologians as examples,

Saint Augustine said, "For He has given them power to become sons of God" (John 1:12). If we have been made sons of God, we have also been made gods by grace." (Exposition on Psalm 50:2)

---

[49] The Garden sanctuary on the Mountain of God featured a threshing floor where life giving seed was separated from worthless chaff. Seed an image representing souls, - Was this where the bride was separated from the rest in eternity?
[50] Jewishnews.co.uk
[51] They should know Jesus' high status above them as the supreme God.

Thomas Aquinas said, "The only begotten Son of God, wishing to enable us to share in his divinity, assumed our nature, so that by becoming man he might make them gods."[52]

And also, "He loved them to the extent that they would be gods by their participation in grace, I said, You are gods" (Psalm 82:6) He has granted to us precious promises, that through these you may become partakers of the divine nature (2 Peter 1:4).

Howard Schwartz in his book, Tree of Souls, The Mythology of Judaism, says,

> "The Souls of the righteous existed long before the creation of the world. God called upon the souls of the righteous, who sat on the council with the Supreme King of Kings, to come together. He took counsel with them before he brought the world into being, saying 'let us make man" (in embodiment form) (Gen 1;26). He asked them if they were willing to be created, and that is how the souls of the righteous, including the souls of Abraham and the patriarchs, came into being."

> "While there is traditions that God took council with the angels or a divine partner such as Adam in creating the world, here the phase "Let us make" from Genesis 1;26 is said to refer to a Council of Souls (nefashot shel Tzaddikim), with whom God consulted before creating the world....Rabbi levi Yitzhak of Berditchev, interprets God's consulting with the souls of the righteous to mean that he asked them if they wanted to be created (Spirits were asked if they wanted to come to earth (created)"[53]

---

[52] Cauley, p.785
[53] Schwartz, Tree of Souls, Mythology of Judaism, Oxford University Press, 2014, p. 161

The Church Father Lactantius (300 AD) said of the two realms,

> *"When all things had been settled with a wonderful arrangement, He determined to prepare for Himself an eternal kingdom and to create innumerable souls, on whom He might bestow immortality. Then He made for Himself a figure endowed with perception and intelligence that is, after the likeness of His own image. So He formed man out of the dust of the ground."*

And Isaiah 6 recalls the prophet Isaiah being caught up to heaven listening into a council, and he heard the voice of the Lord saying, 'Whom shall I send, and who will go for us, then Isaiah says, "Here I am, send me, and he said, Go tell this people..."

It seems we have angels and humans in the council. But what if I propose, that "we" existed before the foundation of the world as spirit's (souls) and agreed to things there[54].

> *"For who has stood in the counsel of the Lord, and has perceived and heard His word? Who has marked His word and heard it?" (Jeremiah 23:18)*

This word counsel in Hebrew is sod. It means a company of persons in sessions, to consult, or a secret. It comes from the Hebrew word *yasad* which means to sit down together, to settle and consult. In this counsel, "we" agreed to the plan that God

---

[54] Humanity's spirits are not indigenous to the earth, but to God's being, this is why they are accountable to His immortal laws, but answerable to them on earth. It is because the earths 'after life' emerged from God's eternal life.

needed (wanted) us to fulfil. We accepted the assignment, and to be born in the time we were born, and to fulfil what we had committed to. Once we accepted this as a part of the counsel of the Lord, it was written in a scroll or book and we were sent to come into the earth, as the word of that scroll made flesh and live it out[55].

I would say the council seems to include both, angels and righteous souls (spirit's) and earth born men.[56]

> *"To the general assembly and church of the first born who are registered in heaven to God the judge of all, to the spirits of just men made perfect." (Hebrews 12:23)*

1 Enoch 62;7-8 - describes the Son of Man together with the congregation of the Elect before their sowing in the earth.

> *"And I swear to you, that there has been no man in his mother's womb, but that already before, even to each one there is a place prepared for repose of the soul, and a measure fixed how much it is intended that a man be tried in this world. Yea children, deceive not yourselves, for there has been previously prepared a place for every soul of man." (2 Enoch 49:3)*

---

[55] Robert Henderson, Operating in the Courts of Heaven, Robert Henderson Ministries, 2014, p. 29.
[56] Adam, Moses, the Seventy Elders all went up the Mountain to have meetings in the Divine Council. The place of men and angels. The Epic of Gilgamesh, Tablet V, reads, 'They stood still and gazed at the forest, They looked at the height of the cedars, they looked at the entrance to the forest. Where Humbaba would walk there was a trail; the road led straight on a path which was excellent. They beheld the cedar mountain, the abode of the gods, Throne-seat of Irnini. From the face of the mountain the cedars' And - 'He went down and trampled through the forest. He discovered the secret abode of the Anunaki, (Gilgamesh snippet, Iraq Museum, Seal 1.1.7.6).

There is an ancient tradition that holds that God took counsel with the souls of the righteous before He created the earth. Specifically named as being present are Adam, Noah, Abraham, and Moses. Enoch said he saw the "first fathers and the righteous who from the beginning dwelt in that place" (1 Enoch 70:4).

The Book of Enoch also describes the naming of the Son of Man from among the righteous, holy, and elect. Enoch was shown that this took place "before the sun and the signs were created, before the stars of heaven were made." The Son of Man was to be a staff to the righteous and the light of the Gentiles, for which purpose He was chosen and hidden. Yet Enoch was assured that he would be revealed to the holy and righteous who would be saved in His name. The name given Him was His Anointed (1 Enoch 48).

The Apocalypse of Abraham gives this description of a Heavenly council,

"And I said: "Primeval One, Strong One, what is this picture of the creature?" And he said to me: "This is my will in relation to that which has a being in the Council, and it became pleasing before me, and then afterwards I commanded them to be through my word. And it came to pass that as many as I had authorized to exist, before portrayed in this picture, and had stood before me precreated, —as many as you have seen,"

From the Manual of Discipline, we learn that the people of Qumran believed themselves to be the stewards of the secrets of the heavenly councils. They wrote of wisdom hidden from the wise, "a fountain of glory (hidden) from the worldly assembly - God has granted these whom He elected as an eternal possession. He has constituted them as an inheritance in the lot of the saints; and he has joined their society with the sons of heaven into a unified congregation and an assembly of saintly fabric."

In the Ascension of Isaiah; an account is given of Isaiah being taken to heaven after the manner of Enoch's experience. There he saw the adversary and his hosts in a great fight that continues here on earth. As he was conducted through the various degrees of heaven, he saw "all the righteous from the time of Adam," and was given a book in which he read "the deeds of the Children of Israel."

In the Secrets of Enoch we read of the Lord instructing Michael to take from Enoch his "earthly garments" to anoint him with oil and then to dress him in the "garments of My glory," that he might enter the heavenly assembly (Secrets of Enoch 22:8–9).

Dexter E. Callender in his book, 'Adam in Myth and History', says, that Adam as a divine gardener was seen as an extension of the divine council,

> "From an ancient Near Eastern perspective, the view of Adam as divine gardener suggests that biblical authors viewed humanity as an earthly extension of the divine council. According to the Eden account, man was immortal (Genesis 2:?7); man had received from deity the sacred "breath of life" (Genesis 2:7); man had been commissioned to perform the work of a god—that is, to till and tend the divine garden. Therefore, as an immortal gardener, man was already "like the gods" prior to partaking of the forbidden fruit.
>
> In Mesopotamian myths, for example, the work of gardening was assigned to lesser members of the divine council. Adam, as an immortal being, clearly reflects

> *the position of the Igigi in Mesopotamian thought. The questions presented to Job by Eliphaz regarding the primal human seem to share this notion"*[57]

> *"Are you the first man who was born? Or were you made before the hills? Have you heard the council of God?" (Job 15:7)*

In Job 15:8, one of Job's friends taunts him, asking if he had sat in the council of God. Effectually he may have been asking, "Do you think yourself so amazing that you sat at the council where plans were made to create the earth?" "Were you present when God said, 'Let us make man in our own image and in our likeness?'

Callender says,

> *"The allusion to the primal human in Job does not give us explicit details concerning his incorporation into the sacred world. It is clear, however, that the idea is present in the reference that the primal human 'listened' in the council of God."?? As a member of God's council, man held a stewardship to "dress" and "keep" the deity's garden (Genesis 2:15). According to the Genesis account, when the man and woman eat from the tree of knowledge, God expels the humans from Eden and assigns the cherubim, other traditional members of the divine council, to "keep" the garden (Genesis 3:24). This move may suggest that in biblical thought "keeping" the garden is a task reserved for members of the divine host. As an immortal subordinate assigned an*

---

[57] Dexter E. Callender Jr., *Adam in Myth and History: Ancient Israelite Perspectives on the Primal Human* (Winona Lake, IN: Eisenbrauns, 2000),

important council task, man, however, eventually appears in the Genesis account as a being very much like the council deities mentioned in Psalm 82 who receive the decree of death:

'I have said, Ye are gods; and all of you are children of the Most High.

But ye shall die like men, and fall like one of the princes.' (Psalm 82:6–7)

'But of the tree of the knowledge of good and evil, thou shalt not eat of it: for in the day that thou eatest thereof thou shalt surely die.' (Genesis 2:17)[58]

And follows on to add,

"The book of Amos declares that "God will do nothing, but he revealeth his secret [sôd] unto his servants the prophets" (Amos 3:7). Though translated as "secret" in the King James Version of the Bible, the noun sôd, in this instance, refers to God's divine council.?? "Generally speaking, the word sôd, translated both 'council' and 'counsel,' is used in the Hebrew Bible to refer to a group or to that which transpires within a given group. When used to signify a group, it is used with reference both to humankind (e.g., Ezek ?3:9) and to the divine realm (e.g., Ps 89:8).[59]

---

[58] Callender Jr., *Adam in Myth and History: Ancient Israelite Perspectives on the Primal Human* (Winona Lake, IN: Eisenbrauns, 2000),

[59] Callender Jr., *Adam in Myth and History: Ancient Israelite Perspectives on the Primal Human* (Winona Lake, IN: Eisenbrauns, 2000),

"This use of Psalm 82:6–7 in the second-century midrash illustrates one of the ways Jewish Theologians reinterpreted this biblical text. When at Mount Sinai Israel "stood before the Lord," the Israelites became the elohim or "gods" mentioned in Psalm 82. The identification of Israel as gods appears in a variety of early Jewish texts:

> *"You stood at Mount Sinai and said, All that the Lord hath spoken will we do, and obey (Exod. 24:7), (whereupon) "I said: Ye are godlike beings" (Ps. 82:6); but when you said to the (golden) calf, This is thy god, O Israel (Exod. 32:4), I said to you, "Nevertheless, ye shall die like men".*[60]

Psalm 82 - Thoughts and Conclusions,

* The text is not talking about God talking to other members of the Trinity, as God is judging the other elohim for corruption.
* God is not going to die like humans (from committing sin).
* Some say, the text and others (Psalm 89) cannot be talking about humans because they don't exist in heaven in councils. But I have shown other-wise with 42 references of created pre-existence, of spirit's (souls) in heaven in ancient texts and early literature, and that Psalm 89 could be one powerful proof among others.
* I have said that there are created angels in the council, and also created pre-existent souls (spirit's) that were in Him (God) before the foundation of the world. The souls become earthly humans; when they enter earthly

---

[60] Jerome H. Neyrey, S.J., "'I Said: You Are Gods': Psalm 82:6 and John ?0," *Journal of Biblical Literature* ?08/4 (?989): 656.

formed bodies at conception, to then be resurrected with glorious bodies in heaven at the end of their lives.

* We are not uncreated God's, we are not angels, but we are a type of elohim, a member of the house-hold of God, to be exalted above the angels to shine the full image of God. This is what the mystery is all about. Our days were written in eternity, fashioned for us, we have eternity written in our hearts for we lived there.
* We were not men floating in space who became Gods, the view of Mormonism.
* In John 10:34-35, Jesus is not saying that he is allowed to call himself the Son of God because every other Jew could. This would undermine Jesus' claim to deity, and being one with the Father. Jesus is saying, 'He is one with the Father the highest Elohim', and this irritates the Jews, but Jesus reminds them that they should know this as they were in the divine council once upon a time as gods.
* Church Fathers and Theologians have interpreted Psalm 82 to speak of men as gods.
* Second-century Midrash illustrates one of the ways Jewish theologians reinterpreted this biblical text. *"You stood at Mount Sinai and said, All that the Lord hath spoken will we do, and obey (Exod. 24:7), (whereupon) "I said: Ye are godlike beings" (Ps. 82:6); but when you said to the (golden) calf, This is thy god, O Israel (Exod. 32:4), I said to you, "Nevertheless, ye shall die like men".*
* Jesus said it straight from his mouth, 'it is written, You are gods.'

"For we will be even gods, if we deserve to be among those whom He declared, 'I have said, You are gods,' and 'God stands in the congregation of the gods.'" (Tertullian 200 AD)

CHAPTER 9 - HYMN OF THE PEARL

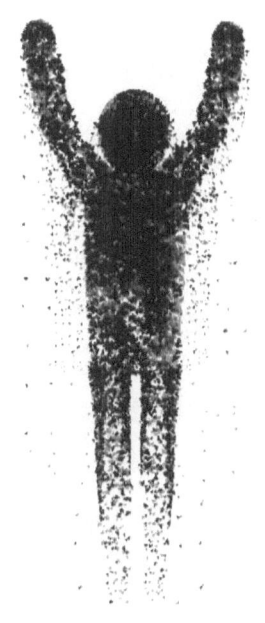

The Hymn of the Pearl is quoted in an apocryphal work entitled, *The Acts of the Apostle Thomas,* probably named after Didymus Judas Thomas, the same Thomas who doubted Christ's resurrection. Many manuscripts of the *Acts* survive, but only two contain the Hymn of the Pearl; One is a Syriac version and the other is in Greek. The original text of the hymn appears to have been written in Syriac, probably in the first or second century A.D.[61] Whatever one thinks of the text, some say there might be a hint of Gnosticism in it, other Scholars say that there is not, and that it is modelled on the prodigal son (Luke 15:11–32) and the pearl merchant (Matt. 13:45–46) parables. I guess it depends on if you believe in the saints' pre-existence in heaven as this will guide how you read it, of which in my studies I do, and have extensively documented this. The text is good to reflect on and see what "truths" are shinning out in the story. It is a story, it's like a parable, but I think there are many hidden truths in it.

Before we read it, I will address a few points, and how it points to heaven, with added Scriptures and some snippets from the text to give us a framework to get the most out of it.

* Some will moan because it is quoted in an apocryphal work, but the 'Hymn' existed outside of that text. It should be considered as a reflection work or commentary of parable truths.

* The son (one of many) is seen (it's hinted) as living in heaven, in the royal house hold in God's palaces.

---

[61] https://byustudies.byu.edu/article/the-hymn-of-the-pearl-an-ancient-counterpart-to-o-my-father/

HYMN OF THE PEARL

* His parents took of his suit and robe before he was sent into the world. This representing his spirit being unclothed of glory, before he entered into his fleshly garment (body).

* This is not strange, as Enoch speaks about this. In the Secrets of Enoch, we read of the Lord instructing Michael to take from Enoch his "earthly garments" to anoint him with oil and then to dress him in the "garments of My glory," that he might enter the heavenly assembly (Secrets of Enoch 22:8–9).

* Before he left, he made an agreement, engraving it upon his mind that he should not forget it. This agreement is the agreement made in the divine council of the assembly of the Saints (Psalm 89) on our scrolls. Rabbi levi Yitzhak of Berditchev, interprets God's consulting with the souls of the righteous to mean, that he asked them if they wanted to be created; (Spirits were asked if they wanted to come to earth (created in flesh bodies)"[62]

* He was sent on a mission to receive a great reward - a pearl. In the world he says, he ceased to know that he was a king's son, and had served their king. I forgot the pearl for which my parents had sent me, and under the weight of their food I sank into deep sleep. The sleep is forgetfulness of who he truly was, a trait of fallenness and living in darkness. The problem is we "see" dimly so we don't remember (1 Cor 13:12). "Shall Your wonder be known in the dark? And Your righteousness in the land of forgetfulness? But to You I have cried out, O

---

[62] Schwartz, Tree of Souls, Oxford Univerity Press, 2014, p. 161

Lord, and in the morning my prayer comes before you." (Psalm 88:12-13).

* In his sleep, he forgets his mission, so his Father sends him a letter, we could say a love letter in the spirit - "From the Father, the King of Kings, and the mother who possesses the East, and the brother who is the second beside us, to our son in Egypt, greetings. Get up and sober up out of your sleep, and listen to the words of this letter. Remember that you are a king's son. You have come under a servile yoke. Think of your suit shot with gold; think of the pearl on account of which you were sent to Egypt, so that your name may be mentioned in the book of the valiant, and you may be an heir with your brother in our kingdom." His awakening from sleep, was awakening in new birth - being born again.

* Some might say, Father, King of Kings, and Mother? Yes, the Father the King, the Holy Spirit - "She is a Tree of Life to those who embrace her; happy are those who embrace her" (Prov 3:18), and the eternal (Son) brother Jesus (Heb 2:10-15).

* And the King sealed (the letter) because of the wicked, children of Babylon, and the tyrannical demons of Sarbug. It flew in form of an eagle, the king of all birds. It flew and landed by me and became entirely speech. And at the sound and sight of it I started up from sleep, took (it), kissed (it) tenderly, and read. And it had written in it just what was written down in my heart. And immediately I remembered that I was a son of kings, and my freedom longed for its kind.

* And at once I directed my course towards the light of the homeland in the East. My parents sent me by their treasurers my shining suit and my long robe. And I did not remember (any more) my brightness. For when I was still a child and quite young, I had left it behind in my father's palaces. And suddenly I saw the suit which resembled (me) as it were in a mirror, and I spied my whole self in it, and I knew and saw myself through it; for we were partially separated from each other, though we were from the same, and again we are one through one form. they gave me precious things, the gorgeous suit which had been skilfully worked in bright colours with gold and precious stones and pearls of brilliant hues. They were fastened above. And the image of the king of kings (was) fully present through the whole (suit). Sapphire stones were set appropriately above.

* "I am (the property) of him who is bravest of all men, for whose sake I was engraved by the father himself." And I myself noticed my stature, which increased in accordance with its impulse. And all the royal movements extended to me. It made haste, straining towards him who should take it from his hand. And love roused me to rush to meet him and receive it. And I reached out, adorned myself with the beauty of its colours, and drew my brilliant garment entirely over me.

But when I had put (it) on I was lifted up to the gate of acknowledgement and worship. And I bowed my head and acknowledged the radiance of the father who had sent this to me; for I had done what had been commanded, and he likewise, what he had promised. And in the gates of the palace, I mingled with those of his dominion. And he rejoiced over me and received me with him in the palace. And all his subjects sing with pleasant voices. And he promised me that I would also be sent with him to the gates of the king, so that with my gifts and my pearl I might together with him appear before the king."

Hymn of the Pearl

"When I was a speechless infant in my father's palaces, resting in the ease and luxury of those who reared me, my parents provided me with means of support and sent me out from the East, our homeland. From the wealth of their treasuries, they put together a pack, large and light, such that I could carry it alone. The pack from above consists of gold and unminted silver from the great treasuries, of chalcedony stones from India and of pearls from the land of the Cushites. And they armed me with diamond which scratches iron. And they took off from me the suit encrusted with stones and shot with gold, which they had made in their love for me, and the robe of yellow colour to match my height. And they made an agreement with me, engraving it upon my mind that I should not forget it, and said: "If you go down to Egypt and fetch from there the single pearl which is there beside the devouring dragon, you shall (again) put on the suit encrusted with stones and the robe which goes over it; and with your brother, our second, become an heir in our kingdom."

I came from the East by a hard and terrible way with two guides, for I had no experience for travelling that way. And I came also along the border-lands of Mesene, where there is the hostel of the oriental merchants, and reached the land of the Babylonians and entered the walls of Sarbug. But when I came to Egypt, the two guides who had travelled with me left me, and

I made straight for the dragon and waited near his lair, watching for him to doze and fall asleep so that I might take away my pearl. And I was alone and foreign in appearance, and I looked strange even to my own (household companions). But there I saw one who was related to me, from the East, one who was free, a graceful and handsome boy, a son of noblemen. He came and associated with me, and I had him as my companion, making him both friend and partner in my journey. And I urged him to be on his guard against the Egyptians and the society of those impure men. But I put on their clothes, so that I might not appear foreign, as one from abroad, in order that I might get the pearl, and so that the Egyptians should not wake up the dragon against me.

But I do not know how they discovered that I was not from their land. But they cunningly devised a trap for me, and I tasted their food. I ceased to know that I was a king's son, and I served their king. I forgot the pearl for which my parents had sent me, and under the weight of their food I sank into deep sleep.

But as I suffered these things my parents also observed it and were sorry for me. And a proclamation was made in our kingdom that everyone should come to our gates. And the kings of Parthia and the potentates and the great ones of the East took a decision about me that I should not remain in Egypt. They wrote me (a letter) and the mighty ones each signed it: "From the father, the king of kings, and the mother who possesses the East, and the brother who is the second beside us, to our son in Egypt, greetings. Get up and sober up out of your sleep, and listen to the words of this letter. Remember that you are a king's son. You have come under a servile yoke. Think of your suit shot with gold; think of the pearl on account of which you were sent to Egypt, so that your name may be mentioned in the book of the valiant, and you may be an heir with your brother in our kingdom."

And the king sealed (the letter) because of the wicked, the children of Babylon, and the tyrannical demons of Sarbug. It flew in form of an eagle, the king of all birds. It flew and landed by me and became entirely speech. And at the sound and sight of it I started up from sleep, took (it), kissed (it) tenderly, and read. And it had written in it just what was written down in my heart. And immediately I remembered that I was a son of kings, and my freedom longed for its kind. And I remembered also the pearl for which I had been dispatched to Egypt. I began to charm the terrible dragon with spells and put him to sleep by uttering the name of my father the names of our second (son) and of my mother, the queen of the East. I stole the pearl, took it away, and returned to my parents. And I took off the dirty garment and left it behind in their country. And at once I directed my course towards the light of the homeland in the East. And I found on the way (the letter) that had roused me. And this, just as it had by its sound raised me up when I slept, also showed me the way by the light (shining) from it; for the royal (letter) of silk stuff was before my eyes. And with love guiding and drawing me, I went past Sarbug. Leaving Babylon on the left I reached great Mesene, which lies on the coast.

My parents sent me by their treasurers my shining suit and my long robe. And I did not remember (any more) my brightness. For when I was still a child and quite young, I had left it behind in my father's palaces. And suddenly I saw the suit which resembled (me) as it were in a mirror, and I spied my whole self in it, and I knew and saw myself through it; for we were partially separated from each other, though we were from the same, and again we are one through one form. Not only (so), but I saw also the treasurers themselves who carried the suit as two, yet one form was present upon both, one royal sign in both. They had wealth and riches in hand, and they gave me precious things, the gorgeous suit which had been skilfully worked in bright colours with gold and precious stones and pearls of brilliant hues. They were fastened above. And the image of the king of kings (was) fully present through the whole (suit). Sapphire stones were set appropriately above.

I saw moreover that movements of knowledge were emitted by the whole, and that it was ready to utter speech. I heard it speak: "I am (the property) of him who is bravest of all men, for whose sake I was engraved by the father himself." And I myself noticed my stature, which increased in accordance with its impulse. And all the royal movements extended to me. It made haste, straining towards him who should take it from his hand. And love roused me to rush to meet him and receive it. And I reached out, adorned myself with the beauty of its colours, and drew my brilliant garment entirely over me.

But when I had put (it) on I was lifted up to the gate of acknowledgement and worship. And I bowed my head and acknowledged the radiance of the father who had sent this to me; for I had done what had been commanded, and he likewise, what he had promised. And in the gates of the palace, I mingled with those of his dominion. And he rejoiced over me and received me with him in the palace. And all his subjects sing with pleasant voices. And he promised me that I would also be sent with him to the gates of the king, so that with my gifts and my pearl I might together with him appear before the king"

Following the view that "the younger son is the Christian who believes in Christ the Son of God and thus becomes a son of God (John 1:12), and that the elder brother is Jesus Christ (Heb. 2:10–15)," The Hymn is presenting the teaching of the

Apostles in Parable form, modelled on the prodigal son (Luke 15:11–32) and the pearl merchant (Matt. 13:45–46).

"But the father said to his servants, bring out the best robe and put it on him, and put a ring on his hand and sandals on his feet." (Luke 15:22)

CHAPTER 10 - DIFFICULT QUESTIONS

We will now reflect on some of the deeper questions people will ask, about the "Treasury of Souls, and our Scroll of Destiny." As for believing that we have existed in heaven first, and have agreed to certain plans for our life, this opens the door for some difficult questions. God's plans for us are good and are not to harm us, but that does not mean our days, lives fashioned for us cannot be difficult, or that God doesn't have a greater plan in our suffering for our (His) glory. We must also note, that we also have an enemy that works against us and through people that affect our lives.

In this book, I have spoken about how Jewish beliefs and Scripture, teach that all souls came out of God (that is they are created finite) and lived in a place before the throne called the "Treasury of Souls". Then when our time comes to be born, according to the timeline before the throne[63], we are drawn out and appointed with our scroll of destiny, that is a scroll with our days fashioned and written on it for us like Jesus also had. And then we are sent to earth to complete our mission on earth.

> *"I come in the volume of the book. It is written of me."*
> *(Psalm 40:7-8)*

> *"The steps of a good man are ordered (established) by the Lord, and he delights in his way." (Psalm 37:23)*

---

[63] The word "Pargod", means a curtain, a veil, and behind this curtain before the throne is the timeline of history. History is written on the curtain, but also behind there are tablets that can be read of historical events. Several Second Temple Jewish materials report that this media of revelation is able to communicate to the seer a disclosure of the 'ages'. For example, 4Q180 1.1-3, 'all ages' are engraved on the heavenly tablets. In the Apocalypse of Abraham it says, you look at the picture and it becomes a scene you become involved in. Enoch was shown the books of heaven, 'O Enoch, look at the books of the tablets of heaven, and read what is written upon them, and learn every individual act. And I looked at everything in the tablets of heaven, and I read everything which was written, and I noted everything." (1 Enoch 81:1-2)

DIFFICULT QUESTIONS

"Bear the record, I know its true, I know where I came from." (John 8:13-14)

One thing with mysteries, if you open them you have to be ready to reflect with compassion and follow through with answers. I saw a post once on Facebook, someone was stating that we agreed to conditions before we came to earth. The post was correct in what it said, but a lady responded in the comments with a difficult reply,

> *"I struggle with this, what about a baby just about to enter the world and is then aborted, what about a person who is born perfect, then something goes wrong and they live their life as a 3-year-old (mental age) all their days being cared for."*

There could be many other bad situations we could list, but I think we get the point. Like I've said, if you open up the mysteries you need to walk carefully, and you need to answer with compassion. In her struggle she gave a brilliant question, now you the reader ask yourself; do you have an answer for what the point is of a soul coming to earth to be killed at birth to go back to heaven is? It's a good question![64]

I am going to try and give some comforting answers and also some insights. Whatever I do say, I will only be grasping some truths, I don't have all the answers and YES, some people's lives are very difficult.

---

[64] These difficult questions do not prove as an argument against God's existence, but challenge us to understand God's character and justified reasons.

God says, that all things work for good who are called by His name, but this doesn't mean it's all easy or a life is full of fun games.

So, let's reflect about the baby questions! Could there be any reasons or any circumstances that a soul would come out of God, live in the Treasury, be appointed with a mission to come to earth, but the mission seems to end at birth (aborted). We could also use the example of miscarriages[65].

Questions we need to reflect on,

* Could there be a greater glory, a greater impact brought forth from a person's evil act (abortion) on an innocent soul? That is God knowing an evil act will happen, as He knows the intentions of the heart. Can God bring a greater good out of it from such a bad situation?

* Would a soul agree to this mission, if his scroll included their full inheritance on earth given to them in heaven, that is their dreams, and on top, the inheritance (rewards) that their life spoke[66] and impacted in the world to others? They were known by people, but maybe never met, but people's hearts were affected from their short existence.

---

[65] If conception comes first, then the soul enters (almost immediately), could 'some' be blocked (stopped) in Heaven in (from) being sent (if the embryo is destroyed/malfunctions to fast), and be sent at another time, or to a different mother? They still get to earth! There are in fact at least three possibilities, (a) God closed Hannah's womb (1 Sam 1:5), (b) Miscarriage - embryo/malfunctions - soul is not sent from Heaven, but at another time, (c) Miscarriage/Abortion - baby/soul dies on earth (and returns to heaven).

[66] Their lives aborted, spoke to those who are alive to reflect deep, and to come to the awareness of the precious value of the soul, of a baby, of a life, and destiny that had a right to unfold. An aborted life speaks to those alive to re-think, re-shape their hearts and world-views.

- No one is saying the loss of a life is good, nor was the cross good for Jesus, but it reaped a greater glory.[67]

  Genesis 4:10, Job 16:18, and Psalm 9:12 say, that one's blood cries out for justice. This is that there is a presence in the earth, in creation that is speaking, crying out, talking to hearts - the blood, the loss of life, the memory. Where there is a cry for justice there is a call for God to move in a greater way.

- The greater the sacrifice a soul endures, for a greater good, the greater the measure of glory they will receive and carry in heaven.

- Could one's mission in these two situations, cry out for laws to be changed to save millions of children, (Abortions), or could miscarriages lead to medical miracles to save many babies?

In none of this am I saying, what has happened is good in "itself", and nothing makes any of the pain go away. But can God have a reason, and can God for a "few" have a short mission for a huge impact?

In Revelation 6:9-16:7, we see the souls that were murdered crying out saying, "how long until there is justice and vindication." - And God says, "rest, and when the number is complete", I will act, like there is a building up of incense before the throne never forgotten.

---

[67] The most spectacular sin in the history of the world was the murder of the perfect Son of God (Jesus), but it was part of God's plan (Acts 4:27-28). In the act, Satan destroyed himself, evil committed suicide against itself, and Jesus triumphed over all evil. God's ways don't always seem like our ways, but He has a perfect purpose for bringing them to pass.

The changing of laws in the earth come because of their "scrolls", their missions. The turning over of abortion laws, the changing of people's hearts, bringing revival, saving others souls, re-shaping minds and the conditions of people's hearts are real outcomes with eternal consequences.

We are also told there is a day of being held accountable, justice will be paid!

Now let's recap before we move on, I'm not saying what unfolded in the earth for these souls is good in itself, and I'm not saying it changes the difficulty. But what if for "some", they agreed to be world changers in a unique way, in a unique mission. And they received a double inheritance, and bring forth fruit through a mystery of ways. Through something wrong happening, their lives were not meaningless or a total waste, from the eyes of eternity but precious.

> *"You intended to harm me, but God intended it for good to accomplish what is now being done, the saving of many lives." (Genesis 50:20)*

* We have options in understanding these things, either God decrees all things, and can bring good out of these bad situations or it's just a bad chance event, or we say, God stands and watches a world where evil just wins.

God decrees our plans, and promises a greater outcome a glory, an overcoming, a victory, of which we agree in part, knowing that life on earth will be affected by actions and situations outside our control, many times evil, but good will overcome evil as we trust Him.

Now what about a person who is born perfect, and gets sick, or end's up with disabilities. Again, we are not saying this is good in itself, or that because a greeter good can come we can understand it. We are saying can we grasp, that God is in it.[68]

I once worked in a supermarket, and this one day a man came down my isle being pushed in a big chair. He was the most handicap person I had ever seen. And the Lord spoke to my heart, "See, he is a suffering servant." I have a whole chapter on this in my book called, *"The Father's Garden"*.[69]

The mentally impaired and severely handicap are very precious to God. Like Jesus was a suffering servant, they too are precious gifts in the earth. Suffering servants, which have to endure much, but oh the weight of glory they will carry.

Their precious souls draw out character traits of deep love and perseverance from careers (parents and others hearts that wouldn't be formed without them. Their souls speak, they draw compassion, they are precious gems, confusing our perceptions

---

[68] "You intended to harm me, but God intended it for good to accomplish what is now being done, the saving of many lives." (Gen 50:20) - 'And that He might make known the riches of His glory on the vessels of mercy, which He had prepared beforehand for glory." (Rom 9:23) - "And we know all things work for good to those who love God, to those who are called according to His purposes." (Rom 8:28) - "You have been grieved by various trails, that the genuineness of your faith, being much more precious than gold that perishes, though it is tested by fire, may be found to praise, honour, and glory at the revelation of Jesus Christ." (1 Pet 1:7-8) - Why was he blind, "Jesus answered, Neither this man nor his parents sinned, but that the works of God should be revealed in him." (John 9:2) - "You who bear the vessels of the Lord...Just as many were astonished at you. So, His visage was marred more than any, and His form than the sons of man." (Isa 52:12,14) -"Indeed we count them blessed who endure. You have heard of the perseverance of Job and seen the end intended by the Lord, that the Lord is very compassionate and merciful." (Jam 5:11) - "For I know the plans I have for you," declares the Lord, "plans to prosper you and not to harm you, plans to give you hope and a future." (Jer 29:11).
[69] Richard Fellows, The Fathers Garden, 2022.

of value and they bring great fruit into the Kingdom. In changing the lives of many through an incredible difficult journey they will be rewarded greatly).

I can remember going to school when I was five in England, there was this handicap girl that started coming. If I'm honest for many months I was terrified of her. I've never seen someone like her since. I used to run out at play-time and sit on top of the climbing frame because I was so sacred of her. This soul, looked Down's-syndrome, but also deaf, and also had eyes the size of golf balls outside her eyelids. I can remember when my mum came to pick me up, this girl had a fascination with my mum's black hair, she loved it. She would always come over and see my mum. Over time I started to get used to this soul, she had a beautiful heart. Some days I could see tears run down her face, she had emotions, a heart, she was precious. I know God would love her, and I know her life has impacted mine ever since.

CHAPTER 11 - THE VEIL OF FORGETFULNESS

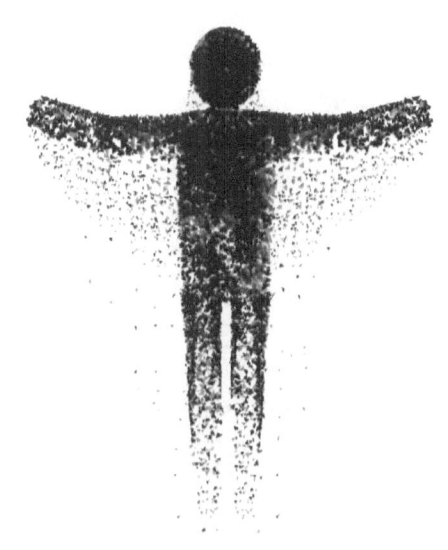

PRE-EXISTENCE – THE HIDDEN MYSTERY

In this Chapter, we will be looking at the concept of the veil of forgetfulness. The claim and concept that God or an angel, the "angel of conception" in heaven, taps just below a baby spirit's nose making them forget their memories, experiences of heaven before they are sent to earth to enter the embryo at conception. This idea, concept is seen in Jewish, Greek, and Christian thought.

From a Jewish lens,

> *"God sits in a circle with many baby spirits that are about to be born. God knows that the babies won't experience the same joy on earth that they experienced in heaven, and He doesn't want them to be dissatisfied. So God touches His finger just below their noses leaving an indentation on their upper lips. This makes them forget the joys of heaven, so that they can adapt to the world into which they are born. When it is a time for a spirit to be born, angels bring us into the womb".*[70]

> *"And angel Lailah, who accompanies the child during pregnancy, teaching it all the secrets of heaven. Then the angel touches the child on the upper lip just as it is born. In an oral variant it is God who touches the child's upper lip and leaves the indentation. This is to make the babies forget all the joy they experienced with God in heaven, for life on earth will be much more difficult."*[71]

Jewish Texts; "B. Niddah 16b, 30b, B. Sandedrin 6a; B. Avot 3;1; Midrash Tanhuma Pekudei 3; Zohar Haddash 68:3; Sefer ha-Zikhronot; Be'er ha-Hasidut 1:216; Avodat Ha - Kodesh.[72]

---

[70] Howard Schwartz, Tree of Souls, Oxford University Press, 2004, p.140
[71] p.140
[72] p.140

From the Christian lens, the Bible,

> *"For now, we see in a mirror dimly, but then face to face. Now I know in part, but then I shall know just as I also am known." (1 Corinthians 13:12)*

> *"Shall Your wonder be known in the dark? And Your righteousness in the land of forgetfulness? But to You I have cried out, O Lord, And in the morning my prayer comes before you." (Psalm 88:12-13)*

The earth is a dark place that we see dimly, Jesus even said, that he came into the world to shine the light, but the darkness did not comprehend it, or receive it (John 1:5;11).

Psalm 23:1-4 depicts the reams of heaven and earth, and the earth being like a shadow of the real,

> *"The Lord is my Shepherd, I shall not want. He makes me lie down in green pastures, He leads me beside the still waters, He restores my soul, He leads me in paths of righteousness for His name's sake. Yea, though I walk through the valley of the shadow of death, I will fear no evil, for You are with me. Your staff and Your rod, they comfort me." (Psalm 23:1-4)*

The next verse, I am not a hundred percent sure in this interpretation, but it is interesting. In Isaiah 14:12 speaking of Lucifer coming down from heaven it says, 'How you are fallen from heaven'. We see this term "fallen" again used in Revelation 3:3 saying to the Church of Sardis, 'Remember therefore whence thou has fallen'. Could the text be saying, remember where you have come from, heaven, where you were sent down, but repent from sinning, as sinning is not your true nature. If you don't, your candle stick will be moved from the light in the City above to outside its light?

> *Remember therefore from whence thou art fallen, and repent, and do the first works; or else I will come unto thee quickly, and will remove thy candlestick out of his place, except thou repent" (Revelation 2:5).*

Does the "Book of Remembrance" in Malachi 3:16 have recorded works we agreed to in eternity?

> *"So, a Book of Remembrance was written before Him, For those who fear the Lord.' (Malachi 3:16)*

From a Gnostic lens; to be clear here, I am not agreeing with the world-view of Gnosticism or using their texts as my belief system, but showing that they also have a concept of the cup of forgetfulness.

> *"The Saviour answered and said unto Mary: "They do not come down in this manner into the world. But the rulers of the Fate, when an old soul is about to come down through them, then the rulers of that great Fate who [are] in the regions of the head of the æons,-- which is that region which is called the region of the kingdom of Adamas, and which is that region which is in face of the Virgin of Light,--then the rulers of the region of that head give the old soul a cup of forgetfulness out of the seed of wickedness, filled with all the different desires and all forgetfulness. And straightway, when that soul shall drink out of the cup, it forgetteth all the regions to which it hath gone, and all the chastisements in which it hath travelled. And of the*

counterfeiting spirit. that cup of the water of forgetfulness becometh body outside the soul, and it resembleth the soul in all [its] figures and maketh [itself] like it, --which is what is called the counterfeiting spirit." (Pistis Sophia)

"That when they offer us the cup of forgetfulness, with one sip we can forget all about heaven, return to earth with its hunger and woe. And then come Yaluham, the receiver of Sabaoth, the Adamas, who handeth the souls the cup of forgetfulness, and he bringeth a cup filled with the water of forgetfulness and handeth it to the soul, and drinks it and forgets all regions and all regions to which it had gone. And they cast it down into a body." (Pistis Sophia)

From a Greek lens; in Greek mythology, Lethe was one of the five rivers of the underworld of hades. Also known as the *Ameles potamos* (river of unmindfulness), the Lethe flowed around the cave of Hypnos and through the Underworld where all those who drank from it experienced complete forgetfulness. Lethe was also the name of the Greek spirit of forgetfulness and oblivion, with whom the river was often identified.[73]

From the lens of Islam,

In Islam, all souls are believed to have been created in adult form (before earthly life) at the same time God created the father of Mankind, Adam. The Quran recounts the story of when the descendants of Adam were brought forth before God to testify that God alone is the Lord of creation and therefore, only He is worthy of worship (Quran chapter 7, verse 172), so that on the Day of Judgement, people could not make the excuse

---

[73] https://en.wikipedia.org/wiki/Lethe

that they only worshipped others because they were following the ways of their ancestors. There are Hadiths that mention that Allah took Adam's offspring from his loins and divided them into those on the right and those on the left. *God then removed the memory of this event from the minds of Mankind (leaving only an innate awareness that He exists and is One, known as the Fitra in Islam) and He decreed at which point each and every human would be born into the physical world.*[74]

So, we can see the belief, the concept is rooted in many cultures, religions and in the Bible. What I find interesting is not many Christians have a clue about this truth. Now I don't believe in Mormonism, and I don't follow their Theology, but it is interesting that they have a great understanding of the veil of forgetfulness.

From the lens of Mormonism, Loss of Premortal Memory at Birth.

Hugh B. Brown

Mortal birth erases recollection of that spiritual pre-existence and the memory of premortal life is as a feeble echo, and yet, as we sometimes sing, "a secret something whispers you're a "stranger here, and we feel that we have wandered from a more exalted sphere." (*Conference Report, October 1963*, pp. 92-93.)

Veil Defined

Neal A. Maxwell

We define the veil as the border between mortality and eternity; it is also a film of forgetting which covers the memories of

---

[74] http://en.wikipedia.org/wiki/Pre-existence#Islam

earlier experiences. This forgetfulness will be lifted one day, and on that day, we will see forever--rather than "through a glass darkly" (1 Cor. 13:12). [From "Patience," *Ensign*, Oct. 1980, p. 31]

The Nature of the Veil

Brigham Young

I say, the greatest good that could be produced by the all-wise Conductor of the universe to His creature, man, was to do just as He has done – bring him forth on the face of the earth, drawing a veil before his eyes. He has caused us to forget everything we once knew before our spirits entered within this veil of flesh. For instance, it is like this: when we lie down to sleep, our minds are often as bright and active as the mind of an angel, at least they are as active as when our bodies are awake. They will range over the earth, visit distant friends, and, for aught we know, the planets, and accomplish great feats; do that which will enhance our happiness, increase to us every enjoyment of life, and prepare us for celestial glory; but when we wake in the morning, it is all gone from us; we have forgotten it. This illustration will explain in part the nature of the vail which is over the inhabitants of the earth; they have forgotten that they once knew. This is right; were it different, where would be the trial of our faith? In a word, be it so; it is as it should be. (*Journal of Discourses*, 1:351-352).

Veil Necessary to Prove Mankind

Joseph Fielding Smith

This mortal existence is conclusive evidence that all who receive it kept their first estate. In our former, or spirit existence, we walked by sight. We were in the presence of both the Father and the Son, and were instructed by them and under their personal presence. In this mortal life, or second estate, the Lord willed that we should walk by faith and not by sight, that we might, with the great gift of free agency, be proved to see if we would do all things whatsoever the Lord our God commanded us. Therefore, he took away from us all knowledge of our spiritual existence and started us out afresh in the form of helpless infants, to grow and learn day by day. In consequence of this we received no former knowledge and wisdom at birth, and, as it is written of the Son of God, who in the beginning made all things, we "received not of the fulness at the first, but received grace for grace." (*Doctrines of Salvation*, 1:60)

Dallin H. Oaks

Our understanding of life begins with a council in heaven. There the spirit children of God were taught his eternal plan for their destiny. We had progressed as far as we could without a physical body and an experience in mortality. To realize a fulness of joy, we had to prove our willingness to keep the commandments of God in a circumstance where we had no memory of what preceded our mortal birth. ("The Great Plan of Happiness," *Ensign*, Nov. 1993, p. 72)

Neal A. Maxwell

It seems clear, not only scripturally but logically, that this second estate could not include either the direct memories or the reference experiences of our first estate. If such were to impinge overmuch upon this second estate, our mortality would not be a true proving ground. (*We Will Prove Them Herewith*, p.3)

Brigham Young

It has also been decreed by the Almighty that spirits, upon taking bodies, shall forget all they had known previously, or they could not have a day of trial-could not have an opportunity for proving themselves in darkness and temptation, in unbelief and wickedness, to prove themselves worthy of eternal existence. The greatest gift that God can bestow upon the children of men is the gift of eternal life; that is, to give mankind power to preserve their identity--to preserve themselves before the Lord. (*Journal of Discourses*, 6:333)

George Q. Cannon

It is not as it was before. We were then in the presence of God. Now there is a veil between us and our Father, and we are left to ourselves, to a certain extent. We are left to be governed by the influences that we invite, and there are any number of evil influences around us, whispering into our ears and hearts all manner of things. If we will open our hearts to receive them or allow them to enter our hearts, we will think evil of our brethren and of our sisters; we will have malice towards them; we will envy them; and we will say bad things about them. God will test us in all this. (*Gospel Truth*, 1:7)

Orson Pratt

What person among all the human family can comprehend what took place in his first existence? No one, it is blotted from the memory, and I think there is great wisdom manifested in withholding the knowledge of our previous existence. Why? Because we could not, if we had all our pre-existent knowledge accompanying us into this world, show to our Father in the heavens and to the heavenly host that we would be in all things obedient; in other words, we could not be tried as the Lord designs to try us here in this state of existence, to qualify us for a higher state hereafter. In order to try the children of men, there must be a degree of knowledge withheld from them, for it would be no temptation to them if they could understand from the beginning the consequences of their acts, and the nature and results of this and that temptation. But in order that we may prove ourselves before the heavens obedient and faithful in all things, we have to begin at the very first principles of knowledge, and be tried from knowledge to knowledge, and from grace to grace, until, like our elder brother, we finally overcome and triumph over all our imperfections, and receive with him the same glory that he inherits, which glory he had before the world was. (*Journal of Discourses,* 15:245-246)

Joseph F. Smith

And yet, to accomplish the ultimatum of his previous existence, and consummate the grand and glorious object of his being, and the salvation of his infinite brotherhood, he had to come and take upon him flesh. He is our example. The works he did, we are commanded to do. We are enjoined to follow him, as he followed his Head; that where he is, we may be also; and being with him, may be like him. If Christ knew beforehand, so did we. But in coming here, we forgot all, that our agency might be free indeed, to choose good or evil, that we might merit the reward of our own choice and conduct. But by the power of the Spirit, in the redemption of Christ, through obedience, we often catch a spark from the awakened memories of the immortal soul, which lights up our whole being as with the glory of our former home. (*Gospel Doctrine*, p.13)

Thomas S. Monson

How grateful we should be that a wise Creator fashioned an earth and placed us here, with a veil of forgetfulness on our previous existence, so that we might experience a time of testing, an opportunity to prove ourselves and qualify for all that God has prepared for us to receive. ("Invitation to Exaltation," *Ensign*, June 1993, p. 4)

Marion G. Romney

To obtain perfection, we had to leave our pre-earth home and come to earth. During the transfer, a veil was drawn over our spiritual eyes, and the memory of our premortal experiences was suspended. In the Garden of Eden, God endowed us with moral agency and, as it were, left us here on our own between the forces of good and evil to be proved--to see if, walking by faith, we would rise to our high potentiality by doing "all things whatsoever the Lord [our] God shall command [us]." (Abr. 3:25.) [From "Prayer Is the Key," *Ensign*, Jan. 1976, p. 2]

M. Russell Ballard

We must understand the basic doctrines and receive the saving ordinances that are essential for our eternal exaltation and happiness. Our present mortal state places a veil of forgetfulness over our minds, allowing us to prove ourselves able to "do all things whatsoever the Lord [our] God shall command" (Abr. 3:25). But even though our present long-range view of eternity is limited, the Lord has not left us without direction. He has provided scriptures and Apostles and prophets through whom he has revealed his plan for our exaltation and eternal life. And we have the Comforter, the Holy Ghost, to guide us. ("Answers to Life's Questions," *Ensign*, May 1995, p. 23)

The Veil is Like Anesthesia

Neal A. Maxwell

In some ways, our second estate, in relationship to our first estate, is like agreeing in advance to surgery. Then the anesthetic of forgetfulness settles in upon us. Just as doctors do not de-anesthetize a patient in the midst of authorized surgery to ask him again if the surgery should be continued, so, after divine tutoring, we agreed to come here and to submit ourselves to certain experiences; it was an irrevocable decision. ("A More Determined Discipleship," *Ensign*, Feb. 1979, p. 70)

The Importance of the Veil

Neal A. Maxwell

We define the veil as the border between mortality and eternity; it is also a film of forgetting which covers the memories of earlier experiences. This forgetfulness will be lifted one day, and on that day, we will see forever--rather than "through a glass darkly" (1 Cor. 13:12).

There are poignant and frequent reminders of the veil, adding to our sense of being close but still outside. In our deepest prayers, when the agency of man encounters the omniscience of God, we sometimes sense, if only momentarily, how very provincial our petitions really are; we perceive that there are more good answers than we have good questions; and we realize that we have been taught more than we can tell, for the language used is not that which tongue can transmit.

We experience this same close separateness when a baby is born, but also as we wait with those who are dying - for then we brush against the veil, as goodbyes and greetings are said--almost within earshot of each other! In such moments, this resonance with realities on the other side of the veil is so real it can he explained in only one way!

No wonder the Saviour said that his doctrines would be recognized by his sheep, that we would know his voice, that we would follow him (see John 10:14). We do not, therefore, follow strangers. Deep within us, his doctrines do strike the promised chord of familiarity and underscore our true identity. Our sense of belonging grows in spite of our sense of separateness, for his teachings stir our souls' awakening feelings within us which have somehow survived underneath the encrusting experiences of mortality.

This inner serenity which the believer knows as he brushes against the veil is cousin to certitude. The peace it brings surpasses our understanding and certainly our capacity to explain. But it requires a patience which stands in stark contrast to the restlessness of the world in which, said Isaiah, the wicked are like the pounding and troubled sea which cannot rest (see Isa. 57:20).

But mercifully the veil is there! It is fixed by the wisdom of God for our good. It is no use our being impatient with the Lord over that reality, for it is clearly a condition to which we agreed so long ago. Even when the veil is parted briefly, it will be on His terms--not ours.

Without the veil, we would lose that precious insulation, thus interfering with our mortal probation and maturation. Without the veil, our brief mortal walk in a darkening world would lose its meaning--for one would scarcely carry the flashlight of faith at noonday and in the presence of the Light of the World!

Without the veil, we could not experience the gospel of work and the sweat of our brow. If we had the security of having already entered into God's rest, certain things would be unneeded;

PRE-EXISTENCE – THE HIDDEN MYSTERY

Adam and Eve did not clutch Social Security cards in the Garden of Eden!

And how could we learn about obedience if we were shielded from the consequences of our disobedience? And how could we learn patience under pressure if we did not experience pressure and waiting?

Nor could we choose for ourselves if we were already in His holy presence, for some alternatives do not there exist. Besides, God's court is filled with those who have patiently overcome--whose company we do not yet deserve.

Fortunately, the veil keeps the first, second, and third estates separate, hence our sense of separateness. The veil avoids having things "compound in one" (2 Neh. 2:11) --to our everlasting detriment. We are cocooned, as it were, in order that we might truly choose. Once, long ago, we chose to come to this very setting where we could choose. It was an irrevocable choice! And the veil is the guarantor that our ancient choice is honoured.

When the veil which now encloses us is no more, time will also be no more (see D&C 84:100). Even now, time is clearly not our natural dimension. Thus, it is that we are never really at home in time. Alternately, we find ourselves impatiently wishing to hasten the passage of time or to hold back the dawn. We can do neither, of course. Whereas the bird is at home in the air, we are clearly not at home in time--because we belong to eternity! Time, as much as any one thing, whispers to us that we are strangers here. If time were natural to us, why is it that we have so many clocks and wear wristwatches?

Thus, the veil stands--not to forever shut us out--but as a reminder of God's tutoring and patient love for us. Any brush against it produces a feeling of "not yet," but also faint whispers of anticipation of that moment when, in the words of today's choral hymn, "Come, Let Us Anew," those who have prevailed "by the patience of hope and the labour of love" will hear the glorious words, "Well and faithfully done; enter into my joy and sit down on my throne" (Hymns, no. 17). [From "Patience," *Ensign*, Oct. 1980, p. 31]

The Veil Will Eventually Be Lifted

LeGrand Richards

When we are born into this world, we only have a vague recollection of our pre-existent life. By the inspiration of the Spirit "we see through a glass darkly" and we "know in part." Ultimately our previous knowledge will be restored to us, when that which is perfect comes, and then we shall know even as also we are known. Here we have the reason why the world did not recognize Jesus when he came in the flesh: "He was in the world, and the world was made by him, and the world knew him not." (John 1:10.)

Ultimately the veil of darkness, or forgetfulness, which deprives us of the recollection of our existence in the spirit world before this earth was made and of the acquaintances we had here, will be lifted. Then we will see as we are seen and know as we are known and as we were known before earth life. (A Marvellous Work and a Wonder, p.281-282)[75]

As we can see, they have an in-depth understanding of the veil of forgetfulness. This is a doctrine that is clearly taught in Jewish Theology and in the Bible, but has seemed to have been poorly picked up on in Christian literature and teaching. You could say it has been seen dimly in a mirror!

---

[75] All above quotes from Mormonism - https://emp.byui.edu/satterfieldb/quotes/Veil%20of%20Forgetfulness.htm

CHAPTER 12 - MY PRIVATE GARDEN

"You are a garden locked up, my sister, my bride, you are a spring enclosed, a sealed fountain." (Song of Solomon 4:12)

Song of Solomon has been interpreted by many Rabbis as speaking of God's love for His creation and people[76]. In that light the words of Solomon will be interpreted here as the words of God. The phase, "Song of Songs", often given to the book means the greatest of songs, and the Jews refer to it as the Holy of Holies[77]. The book is profound, but also graphic in deep love and intimacy.

We were chosen in Him from the foundation of the world to come forth and were created in heaven and placed in the Garden, and God came and met with us. The Garden, the sacred sanctuary, throne room, was God's bedchamber where He embraced us in His love. In that moment, God's presence, light and mist of His glory entered and covered us soaking into our souls and we were united to Him as His bride. God set a seal upon our hearts for eternity (8:6), and in this marriage process we became one body.

God's face (My beloved) is white and ruddy, chief among ten thousand (5:10) and the Spirit of God was hovering over the face of the waters (Gen 1:2). God was on His mercy seat, shadowing over the Ark of the Cherubim with the Water of Life. The Spirit of God was like a fountain, spring, reservoir of water flowing out of God. The Spirit of God vibrated and breathed us out

---

[76] In the context of Song of Songs, that being between God and His people, we must take note it also takes the image of the body (a woman) as the Sanctuary Temple before the throne. One must work with these two images interchanging carefully, His love upon the entering of the womb of creation, the Garden, and upon the love of His people.

[77] Why is the book called the Holy of Holies? It is because it is describing the birth of creation in the womb of God, the most intimate and holy act that has ever happened in a realm of time.

and we were birthed in the mist of glory, as the mystery, the hidden Church.

The word "Beresheet" (the first word in the Bible) speaks of the events of the entire seven-day creation week. The Hebrew letters of the first word, Beresheet; "In the beginning" come from two words, 'brit', meaning "Covenant", and 'esh', meaning "Fire". The Creation Covenant was the Covenant of Fire. The word 'brit', means to cut or join together and speaks of a marriage covenant and the forming of a house-hold, that being the family of God.

> *"By Wisdom is a house built, by understanding it is made secure, and by knowledge its rooms are filled with all kinds of costly, pleasant possessions." (Proverbs 23:3-4)*

God hovering over the waters, the Spirit over the face of the deep, is God's face overshadowed by the Spirit vibrating, fluttering, breathing over the darkness. This was the sanctuary of darkness under the shadow of God. Then God shone upon us the light of the world, and we came into visibility. The earth was without form and void, it was like a wilderness before "we" appeared. We dwelled in the thick darkness, like little candles until God shone upon us in the heavenly sanctuary. But God was there, for He dwells in darkness (1 Kings 8:12).

When we felt His light, deep called to deep, and a covenant was made. Now darkness is not a principle opposed to the light, but merely the absence of light. Then God shone upon us, the light of the world and we were illumed with visibility and awe. God saw our "form" (spirit) and spoke to us,

"O my dove, in the cleft of the rock in the secret place of the steep pathway. Let me see your 'form', let me hear your voice, for your voice is sweet and your form is lovely." (Song of Solomon 2:14)

"Who is this coming out of the wilderness, like Pillars of smoke, perfumed with myrrh and frankincense..." (Song of Solomon 3:6)[78]

God says, 'You are My private Garden, my treasure, my bride'. Again, we are being taken back to the Garden in eternity revealing the hidden mystery. Those in the Garden are those who were chosen in Christ before the foundation of the world, God's holy seed and a pure gift to the eternal Son. As we have seen in earlier chapters, the Garden symbolizes, not only a woman's body (vagina/womb), but those inside the Garden as being in a private garden[79]. The Garden in a virginity state is revealing that their pureness had not been given to another. Inside the garden was the pure bride, in the perfect soil, growing in love.[80]

Amazingly the early Church Father Clement of Alexandria saw this and said, "God knew us before the foundation of the world, and chose us for our faithfulness even at that time. Now we have become babes to fulfil the plan of God."

---

[78] According to the most natural reading of the Hebrew text, the land was simply an "uninhabitable" or "inhospitable" stretch of "wasteland. Through the hand of God, the "wasteland", "wilderness" is about to become the "promised land Paradise with the children of God." This also hints back to Genesis 1:2.
[79] In the womb.
[80] The Garden Temple was called the bedchamber. The place of a sacred copulation (zivvug ha-kodesh), an image of a sacred marriage (hiero gamos). The bride impressed on His body like a seal imprinted upon a page (8:6).

God's private garden was the secret place, under the shadow of God's wings the Ark (ovaries). In Palestine, rock walls surrounded gardens and vineyards in order to prevent strangers from intruding. Only the lawful owners of the garden could enter.[81]

"A garden enclosed, is my sister, my spouse, a spring shut up, a fountain sealed. Your plants are an orchard of pomegranates." (Song of Solomon 4:12)

The term my sister, is one by birth, by being a partaker of the divine nature, for we came from God. My bride, is one in love joined by scared ties. What God joins together becomes one flesh. When the Father, through the Holy Spirit brought the eternal Son forth, we were soon created under him and became the body of Christ. We were betrothed to Christ and yoked to Him and become one.

> *"For the husband is head of the wife, as also Christ is head of the church, and He is the saviour of the body." (Ephesians 5:23)*

Adding the Hebrew letter 'num' (seed) to 'ehd' (mist) forms 'Eden" - the place where water and seed originated and become intimate.[82]

When Christ entered the Garden under the throne, His private Garden, secret place, His presence filled us and we encountered His overwhelming, intoxicating love. So overwhelming that it took our breath away, and fulfilled us to the highest degree. We surrendered in His presence and joined in His love, in

---

[81] Joseph Dillow, Intimacy Ignited, NavPress, 2004, p. 151
[82] Dye, p.41

an act of worship and become one with Him. This was our eternal home, and those in Christ where there!

> *"Your lips, O my spouse, drip as the honey comb, honey and milk are under your tongue. And the fragrance of your garments is like the fragrance of Lebanon." (Song of Solomon 4:11)*

As we stood worshipping God in love our garments our glorious bodies gave off a fragrance pleasing to God, and they still do to this day as we walk in holiness (2 Cor 2:15).

> *"Your shoots (plants) are an orchard of pomegranates with pleasant fruit, fragrant henna with spikenard." (Song of Solomon 4:13)*

In verse 13, when it says that "shoots" compose her garden a different Hebrew word is used, Pardes - a word that means Paradise. This garden Paradise is filled with fruit and spices (us).

We then read,

> *"Awake, O north wind and come O south and blow upon my garden that its spices may flow out. Let my beloved come into his garden and eat it pleasant fruits." (Song of Solomon 4:16)*

But let us not go to fast, there is more imagery to be seen before 'we' came forth. Let's take a few steps back, a call goes out form the stirring of God's heart, 'Awake, O north wind and south' this is describing the winds of passion the longing for the Spirit of God to be intimate with creation. The verse is speaking on many levels, speaking about God intimately breathing life upon the sanctuary and then conceiving His bride and making a Covenant. God's breath is impregnated with creative power. We must pick up that there is the womb of creation, the sanctuary that is pictured as a woman, and also the bride of God to be conceive as a woman the people of God. For we know that the whole of creation has been groaning as in pains of childbirth (Rom 8:22). God made a Covenant with both as seen in Hosea 2:20-23 and Hebrews 13:20.

Dillow says,

> *"In Palestine, the north wind brings clear weather and removes clouds, and the south wind brings warmth and moisture. When these winds blow across a garden, the combination of sun, rain, and warmth promotes growth. The winds of passion stimulate her garden with caresses to promote growth of her sexual passion."*[83]

I would also add, and the opportunity to conceive and have souls grow inside the Garden.

The Congregation is the community of the elect. On a side note; I have finally come to understand what Lucifer wanted by coming up into the Congregation of the North, he wanted to rule over us.[84]

In the Dead Sea Scrolls (4Q 418), Adams, descendants, who will obey are described as "Walking in an eternal plantation".

---

[83] Dillow, p. 152

[84] Scripture speaks of believers as the congregation, 'The congregation of the Lord (Mal 2:5), The congregation of Israel (Exod 12:3), The congregation of the righteous (Psalm 1:5), The congregation of the mighty (Psalm 82:1), The congregation of the Saints (Psalm 89:5), The assembly of the elders (Psalm 107:32), The assembly of the people of God (Judges 20:2), The assembly of the Saints (Psalm 98:7), The assembly of the upright (Psalm 11:1)'. p.99.

The main task of this dwelling is image bearing reflecting the praises of all creation back to its maker.[85]

The Temple on Zion was a well-watered garden, and a spring that never fails. Those in eternity in the Garden were a well-watered garden with a spring, reservoir that brought the water and mist of God bringing life and pleasure and intimacy.

> *"The Lord will guide you continually and satisfy your soul in drought, and strengthen your bones. You shall be like a watered garden, and like a spring of water, whose waters do not fail." (Isaiah 58;11)*
>
> *You are a garden locked up, my sister, my bride, you are a spring enclosed, a sealed fountain." (Song of Solomon 4:12)*

In the ancient Aramaic commentary of the Targum, for example, the images of the "locked garden" and the "sealed spring" are interpreted as follow: "You women who are married are chaste like a chaste bride, and like the Garden of Eden, which no one has permission to enter save the righteous. Your virgins are sealed thus they are like the spring of living water."[86]

The Garden is symbolic of the sanctuary, but also of a woman's vagina, of which from the act of marriage (betrothed) to God, we came forth and are inside the Garden (Paradise) until we are sent to the earth. The Garden is sealed, it is an enclosed garden, a sealed fountain. The fountain, well, spring is the Spirit of God's waters flowing, but it also is used to symbolizes when in deep intimacy, the fluids, at first a mist, and then an over

---

[85] Dye, p 43
[86] Philip S. Alexander, The Targum of Canticles: Introduction, Translation, Apparatus and Notes, The Aramaic Bible: The Targums 17A (Wilmington, DE: M. Glazier/T&T Clark International, 2003), 141

flowing like waters that stream from a woman's vagina. This is the spring of pleasure that runs out when the seal is broken and awakened. The word 'hovered' over the waters in Genesis 1:2 in Hebrew, means, to 'vibrate', and God was vibrating over the ground, and a mist came up and watered the inside of the Garden. This is symbolic of a woman's vulva and clitoris[87] being breathed on, the vibration trigger's a mist, that starts to stream like waters.

The Hebrew verb, *m'rachefet*, to sweep or flutter, is "vibration", movement, and is like fluttering packets of energy shimmying the dance of becoming. The vibration and frequency dance and then plants a record of a Testimony inside the womb (garden sanctuary)[88]. In intense intimacy[89] orgasm explodes[90] and conception can take place, and it did when we came forth[91]. Many waters cannot quench love...

Both Song of Solomon 2:16 and 6:3 describe the male as he who, "Grazes among the Lotus".[92]

"Set about with lilies (or lotus)" - pubic hair that guards and graces the "banquet bowl" of the vulva.

---

[87] The Clitoris triggers the hormone DMT to be released from the Pineal Gland that opens spiritual states of awareness. We came into existence in an atmosphere of spiritual bliss.

[88] Testimonies, the souls and scrolls of those brought forth out of the DNA of God.

[89] That is in sexual intercourse between and man and woman conception is birthed.

[90] God created sex and orgasm to be the climax of His creation. Deep calls to deep in climax. Orgasm reflects being flooded with the highest presence, breathless in pleasure. Husbands love your wives as Christ loves the Church. Total union of love, one flesh.

[91] A Woman can orgasm in childbirth, and we were brought forth in bliss.

[92] Dr. Kevin Leman, says, 'Many teachers believe that these passages directly relate to oral sex.' - 'Sheet Music, Uncovering the Secrets of Sexual Intimacy in Marriage, Tyndale, 2008, p.113.

"Your Naval is like a round goblet which never lacks wine" (7:1-2) - the Navel is usually translated 'vulva', and the description that it never lacks wine speaks of it as a source of sexual pleasure and moistness. It is said to look like a round goblet or bowl in the shape of a half moon.[93]

This is also seen in Proverbs 5:15-19, that the waters flow from a well. But these waters are only for a husband and wife and not to be shared with strangers.

> *"Drink water from your own cistern and running water from your own well. Should your fountains be dispersed abroad, streams of water in the streets? Let them be only your own and not for strangers with you. Let your fountain be blessed and rejoice with the wife of your youth. As a deer and graceful doe, let her breasts satisfy you at all times, and always be enraptured with her love." (Proverbs 5:15-19)*

The ancient Jewish text, The Holy Letters, sees sex as a mystical experience of meeting God. Through the act of intercourse, they become partners in the act of creation. This is the mystery of what the sages said, 'When a man unites with his wife in holiness, the Shekinah is between them in the mystery of man and woman.'[94]

In the encounter in eternity, we have been chosen as a bride adorn with jewels, and as fruit of the Lord sown into the Garden, it will spring forth righteousness and praises before the nations.

---

[93] Robert Gordis, The Song of Songs, New York; The Jewish Theological Seminary of America, 1954, p.26
[94] Nahmanides, The Holy Letters, p.60

> *"I will greatly rejoice in the Lord, my soul shall be joyful in my God. For he has clothed me with the garments of salvation. he has covered me with a robe of righteousness. As a bridegroom decks himself with ornaments, and as a bride adorns herself with her jewels. For the earth brings forth its bud, as the garden causes the things that are sown in it to spring forth. So the Lord God will cause righteousness and praises before the nations." (Isaiah 61:10-11)*

We are the bride of Christ, hidden in the cleft of the Rock[95], sent down to earth to show our love and faithfulness trusting by faith God's purpose for us walking holy and blameless in the earth as one just passing through. We are being transformed from glory to glory, and will be resurrected at the end, and go back into our home in glorious bodies to be in the eternal city. In our transformation we will become a pure elohim united in God's love.

The Church Father Cyprian (250 AD), said, "If His Church is a garden enclosed, and fountain sealed, how can he who is not in the Church enter into the same garden or drink from its fountain". - The Church is the apples inside the garden.

---

[95] Song of Song 2:14 - "cleft of the Rock"; the word "cleft" is described as a narrow opening, a hollow between two parts. Caves in the ancient world represented the inner sanctuary of a temple, where Heaven & earth became one. Again, we see the symbolism of a bride's body, the enclosed Garden, entered through the vagina (dark cave opening, between two parts) where in intimacy the act of betrothal takes place.

CHAPTER 13 - TRANSFORMING ELOHIM

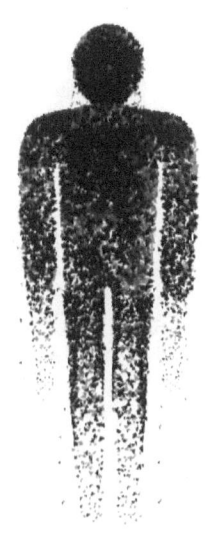

In this journey of sanctification and from going from glory to glory we are transforming into a glorious elohim. For many, we have not unlocked who we truly are or stepped into the abilities of our priestly and kingly callings. There are a few in the earth, hidden ones, who have been caught up to heaven and are being trained under God Himself and are being quickened in this process. They can instantly travel in the spirit anywhere on the globe in the Lord's light (spirit) (Ezek 8:3). They can battle in the heaven's and take down thrones, have ranks of angels placed under their authority, and even explore Eden in heaven, and meet the Father face to face. Some may think we will do this when we die, but no, these ones are doing it now, and it comes from a surrendered life[96]. For all will not be the same, as one star differs from another in glory.

In time, they will be transformed into a created elohim, who will be able to govern over planets[97], galaxies, heavenly cities, and the earth under God's authority (Luke 19:17).

Is this some sort of heresy? No, the early Church Fathers didn't think so, nor do the ones doing it.

---

[96] There are a few in the earth that will not taste death. They have spent so many hours up in Heaven that they have taken on, tasted the powers of the age to come (Heb 6:5), and have aligned with the record of eternal life throughout their DNA. 'For this corruptible must put on incorruption, and this mortal must put on immortality' (1 Cor 15:53). Yes, it can be done while on earth, these ones will be like Enoch, when their mission is complete, they will go into Heaven and not come back, but death will not be the cause of their departure.

[97] When Christ returns there will be a renewal of creation, a new earth & Heavens. The veil will be gone, but there will still be celestial lands in the Heavens to govern. Some will rule on earth, others in the Heavens. There is the New Jerusalem city, thrones/bases in the Heavens (planets), and other cities on earth in the Kingdom to govern. I think maybe the New Jerusalem City will come down and hover over the earth like a Mountain (Rev 21).

"We with unveiled faces beholding the glory of the Lord, are being transformed into the same image" (2 Corinthians 3:17-18)

The early Church Father, Justin Martyr (150 AD) said,

"But as my discourse is not intended to touch on this point [the fall of Satan], but to prove to you that the Holy Ghost reproaches men because *they were made like God, free from suffering and death*, provided that they kept His commandments, and were deemed deserving of the name of His sons, and yet they, becoming like Adam and Eve, work out death for themselves; let the interpretation of the Psalm be held just as you wish, yet thereby it is demonstrated that **all men are deemed worthy of becoming 'gods,' and of having power to become sons of the Highest**; and shall be each by himself judged and condemned like Adam and Eve."[98]

Justin Martyr in his Dialogue with Trypho states, that the Christians are the "true children of God, because it was affirmed prophetically by the Spirit, when it said they are the sons of the highest" - an illusion to Psalm 82:6.

The early Church Father Tertullian (160 AD) said,

*"Truth, however, maintains the unity of God in such a way as to insist that **whatever belongs to God Himself belongs to Him alone**. For so will it belong to Himself if it belongs to Him alone; and therefore, it will be impossible that another god should be admitted, when it is permitted to no other being to possess anything of God. Well, then, you say, we ourselves at that rate possess nothing of God. But indeed, we do, and shall continue to do— only it is from Him that we receive it, and*

---

[98] Justin Martyr, Dialogue with Trypho 124

*not from ourselves. For **we shall be even gods**, if we shall deserve to be among those of whom He declared, I have said, You are gods, and, God stands in the congregation of the gods. **But this comes of His own grace, not from any property in us, because it is He alone who can make god's.**"*[99]

Irenaeus of Lyons (130 AD), states, "God stood in the congregation of the gods, He judges among the gods. He refers to the Father and Son, and those who have received the adoption, for these are the Church. For she is the synagogue of God."

The early Church Father Origen (185 AD) said,

"Now the God of the universe is the God of the elect, and in a much greater degree of the saviours of the elect, then He is the God of these beings who are gods. Now we have these comments that we may flee being men with all strength and hasten to become gods.

Patristic Theologian Hamilton Hess notes, "Athanasius of Alexandria in his Festal letters as saying, "God became man so that we might become God."[100]

Saint Macarius wrote, "that those Christians who struggle and conquer are kings and lords and gods."[101]

Saint Methodius (311 AD) said, "And therefore the church swells and travails in birth until Christ is formed in us, so that each saint, by partaking of Christ, has been born a Christ."

---

[99] Tertullian, Against Hermogenes
[100] Marty Cauley, Misthological Models Part 5: A Panoramic View of New Jerusalem, Independently Published, 2022, p.785
[101] The Firty Homilies, Homily 27

Saint Gregory Nazianzus argued "that the root of a person's true greatness and calling lay in being called a god."

Saint Basil said, "the goal of our calling is to become god like. Human beings are nothing less than creatures that have been ordered to become gods."

Saint Peter Damacus, - "No activity or place on the whole creation can prevent us from becoming what God from the beginning has wished us to be, that is to say, according to His image and likeness, gods."

Saint Augustine said, "For He has given them power to become sons of God" (John 1:12) If we have been made sons of God, we have also been made gods by grace."[102]

Thomas Aquinas said, "The only begotten Son of God, wishing to enable us to share in his divinity, assumed our nature, so that by becoming man he might make them gods."[103]

And also, "He loved them to the extent that they would be gods by their participation in grace, I said, You are gods" (Psalm 82:6) He has granted to us precious promises, that through these you may become partakers of the divine nature (2 Peter 1:4)".[104]

According to Eastern Christian teaching, Theosis is very much the purpose of life.

Theologian Robert M. Brown agrees that the early Church Fathers taught that we could become gods, but he nicely explains why this teaching is not the same as what Mormons teach.

> *"Establishing that the early church fathers taught a doctrine of deification does not, in and of itself, show that the Mormon doctrine of exaltation is a restoration*

---

[102] Exposition on Pslam 50:2)
[103] Cauley, p.785
[104] Commentary of Gospel of John

of ancient truth. One must compare the substance of the two doctrines in order to determine if they are at all close in meaning. To that end, I will list the specific doctrinal elements of the Mormon doctrine of exaltation that orthodox Christians consider erroneous:

1st *God has not always been God; it is not true that he has been God from all eternity (though he may have existed from all eternity, he has not always existed as God).*

2nd *God was once a man like us before becoming God our Heavenly Father.*

3rd *God became God and is an exalted man, an exalted being.*

4th *Human beings are the spirit offspring of God, our Heavenly Father, and of Heavenly Mother. We lived in heaven with these heavenly parents before becoming physical beings here on earth.*

5th *We became human beings precisely so that we would have the opportunity to attain exaltation just as God did.*

6th *Human beings can become "gods" in the sense of becoming exalted beings fully like Heavenly Father in all essential respects, just as he did before us.*

7th *As exalted beings or gods, we can become creators and have all the power, glory, dominion, and knowledge that God the Father has (in the worlds we create).*

8th *Read through the quotations from the church fathers found in LDS articles defending their doctrine of exaltation and you will quickly see that the church*

> *fathers affirmed none of these seven doctrinal elements. Readers lacking some background in the theology of the church fathers might easily get confused by such quotations. However, you will not find in any of the church fathers' writings them affirming, for example, that God the Father was a man who progressed to Godhood, or that God has not always been God, or that the spirits of human beings are uncreated and eternal gods in embryo. The core premises of Joseph Smith's doctrine of exaltation are completely absent from the corpus of the church fathers' writings as a whole."[105]*

I agree with Robert M. Brown on all points, except two[106], and that is we did live in heaven first as spirits, and this we have seen extensively documented in other chapters of this book. But true we are not uncreated eternal gods in embryo. But we are created sons of God that will reflect our true image and likeness as a perfected transformed elohim.

Clement of Alexandria (150 AD) said that, "He who obeys the Lord and follows the prophecy given him becomes a god while moving about in the flesh."[107]

Cryril of Alexandria tells us, "He came down into our condition solely in order to lead us to his divine state."

Theosis Theology

From the writings of many of the Church Fathers we can see that they taught the Theology of Theosis. This is the doctrine of

---

[105] https://mit.irr.org/mormon-doctrine-of-becoming-gods-what-about-early-church-fathers
[106] 4 And 5 - but not eternal
[107] Stromata 716,101

finite deification. Church Fathers and Theologians throughout the ages have pointed to a number of Scriptures that they believe teach this doctrine. We will go over the main ones here.

- *"I said, You are god's" - (Psalm 82)*

- *"But we all, with unveiled face, beholding as in a mirror the glory of the Lord, are being transformed into the same 'image,' from glory to glory, just as by the Spirit of the Lord." (2 Corinthians 3:18)*

- *"By which have been given to us exceedingly great promises, that through these you may be partakers of the divine nature, having escaped the corruption that is in the world through lust." (2 Peter 1:4)*

- *"For our citizenship is in heaven from which we also eagerly wait for the savoir, the Lord Jesus Christ, who will transform our lowly body that it may be conformed to His glorious body." (Philippians 3:20-21)*

- *"The disciple is not above his Master, but everyone who is perfect shall be as his Master." (Luke 6:40)*

- *"To him who overcomes, I will grant to sit with Me on My throne, as I also overcame and sat down with My Father on His throne." (Revelation 3:21)*

The last two, I will add some comments, and explanations,

John 17:22, speaks of us returning to glory, from where we came. When the righteous die, their spirit returns to heaven in glory. The nature of glory is the reflection of God.

- *"And the glory which You gave Me I have given them, that they may be one just as We are one." (John 17:22)*

- *"Therefore, since we are the offspring of God, we ought not to think that the Divine Nature is like gold or silver or stone, something shaped by art and man's devising." (Acts 17:29)*

1 Corinthians 15:41-42, speaks about there being different degrees of glory, one of the sun, the moon and the stars. Matthew 13:43, also says, that the righteous will shine forth like the sun in the Kingdom of their Father. It is my opinion, that this teaches that we are eternally saved, but it does matter how we walk in this life in our transformation.

- *"There is one glory of the sun, another glory of the moon, and another glory of the stars, for one star differs from another in glory. So also, is the resurrection of the dead. The body is sown in corruption, it is raised in incorruption. (1 Corinthians 15:41-42)*

Remember what Saint Macarius said, "that those Christians who struggle and conquer are kings, and lords and gods."

The Role of Grace in Theosis

In distinction to the Son who is God by nature, together with the Father & Spirit, believers are adopted and become gods by grace. One must always keep the distinction between the eternal Creator and His finite creation apart (Rom 1:25). We will never become one of the members of the Trinity, but we will be a god of the energies of His nature, that reveals the full Image of God as God sustains us as immortals.

Leonid Outspensky writes,

> *"Orthodox theology insists on the uncreated character of grace and defines it as a natural procession, as the energy characteristic of the common nature of the three divine persons. By the energies, man surpasses the limits of the creature and becomes a 'partaker' of the divine nature."*[108]

This needs to be explained a little clearer, God's eternal essence, which is incomprehensible is different and distinct from God's energies. For example, the sun's essence and energies are distinct. The suns essence and its rays are different.

I end this Chapter with the words of the Church Father Hippolytus (150 AD) 'If man becomes immortal, he will also become a god. Made partaker of the divine nature."

---

[108] L. Outspensky, Theology of the Icon, Seminary Press, 1978, p. 29

CHAPTER 14 - ONE STAR DIFFERS

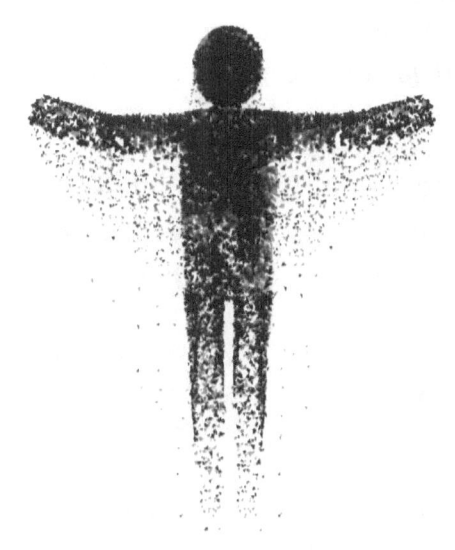

In this Chapter, we will be looking at the meaning, and most accurate translation of 1 Corinthians 15:35-49, Speaking about the different degrees of glory one may attain in the resurrection. We will be focusing greatly on the last verse, 49, and it's wording in nearly all the ancient manuscripts.

The Resurrection Body

"³⁵ But someone will ask, "How are the dead raised? With what kind of body will they come?" ³⁶ How foolish! What you sow does not come to life unless it dies. ³⁷ When you sow, you do not plant the body that will be, but just a seed, perhaps of wheat or of something else. ³⁸ But God gives it a body as he has determined, and to each kind of seed he gives its own body. ³⁹ Not all flesh is the same: People have one kind of flesh, animals have another, birds another and fish another. ⁴⁰ There are also heavenly bodies and there are earthly bodies; but the splendor of the heavenly bodies is one kind, and the splendor of the earthly bodies is another. ⁴¹ The sun has one kind of splendor, the moon another and the stars another; and star differs from star in splendor. ⁴² So will it be with the resurrection of the dead. The body that is sown is perishable, it is raised imperishable; ⁴³ it is sown in dishonor, it is raised in glory; it is sown in weakness, it is raised in power; ⁴⁴ it is sown a natural body, it is raised a spiritual body. If there is a natural body, there is also a spiritual body.⁴⁵ So it is written: "The first man Adam became a living being"; the last Adam, a life-giving spirit. ⁴⁶ The spiritual did not come first, but the natural, and after that the spiritual. ⁴⁷ The first man was of the dust of the earth; the second man is of heaven. ⁴⁸ As

was the earthly man, so are those who are of the earth; and as is the heavenly man, so also are those who are of heaven. ⁴⁹ And just as we have borne the image of the earthly man, so shall we bear the image of the heavenly man." (1 Corinthians 15:35-49)

Many translations of this section of Scripture read verse 49 as, "And just as we have borne the image of the earthy man, so shall we bear the image of the heavenly man." But this is not the most accurate translation of nearly all the ancient manuscripts, and many Scholars know this, but many don't like what it concludes too. Nearly all the ancient manuscripts read, "And just as we have borne the image of the earthly man, let us bear the image of the heavenly man." This makes a huge difference.

The verse is not saying, we will just bear Christ's image, it is saying, "let us bear", let us conform in yielding to the life of the heavenly man. We must strive to put on Christ and bear Christ's image now morally, if we wish to bear it fully in heaven. To the degree you bear His image, is the degree of glory you will shine in heaven[109]. For not all stars have the same splendour, nor do all stars shine the same (verse 41). Let us bear, is a command to shine forth the image of Christ now in this world, to put Him on. Attending to a high degree of glory, like a star, moon or sun, depends on our own efforts of yielding into the heavenly man. Those whose works are all burnt up at the bema-seat of Christ, most likely will not shine (1 Corinthians 3:15) .

The early Church Father Tertullian said, "Let us bear as a precept, not, "we shall bear in the sense of promise."

---

[109] This is not 'Works Salvation', but Kingdom Santification transformation.

When the Apostle Paul says - "Their glory is their shame" (Philippians 3:19) he is describing the state of some believers who shine little, their glory shows they did not transform on earth. They will be loved in heaven, but there will be a cost.

The ending of 1 Corinthians 15, verse 58 (Sun, Moon & Stars - Chapter) says,

> *"Therefore, my beloved brethren, be steadfast, immovable, always abounding in the work of the Lord, knowing that your labour is not in vain in the Lord."*

Marty Cauley, makes the point,

> *"Why would Paul say, our work is not in vain (1 Cor 15:58) if our bearing the heavenly image is not impacted by our work (1 Cor 15:49)*[110]

Daniel 12:1-3 says,

> *"And at that time your people shall be delivered, everyone who is found written in the book. And many of those who sleep in the dust of the earth shall awake, some to everlasting life, some to shame, and everlasting contempt. Those who are wise shall shine like the firmament, and those who turn many to righteousness like the stars forever and ever." (Daniel 12:1-3)*

Daniel is saying, when the time for resurrection comes for his people, all those found in the book of life (only believers)

---

[110] Marty Cauley, Redeemed Bodies Versus Glorified Bodies: Stars Differs from Star in Glory, 2022, Kindle.

will awake, some shall shine like stars, but also some will not, but be dim in shame.

> *"And now, little children, abide in Him, that when He appears, we may have confidence and not shrink back ashamed before Him at His coming" (John 2:28)*

Donna Rigney in her book, 'The Glory Revealed', shares a heaven encounter she had where she spoke to a lady in heaven in plain clothes, the lady told her,

> *"I ruled harshly and bitterly on earth, that is why my dress is plain. I did not let His love pour out of me. She was rewarded, but could not serve in the Courts of the Lord, her reward was a different degree."*[111]

The Church Fathers, interpretations on, 'One star differs from another in glory',[112]

> *Augustine affirms that not all believers, even though they have eternal life, will attain to the brightest star of glory in 1 Cor 15:49 – "For star differs from star in brightness, so also the resurrection of the dead. It is therefore good for man so to be, yet star differs from star in glory, so also is the resurrection of the dead. These are different merits of the saints."*

---

[111] Donna Rigney, Gory of God Revealed, Its Supernatural, 2021
[112] Thankful for Marty Cauleys references for the Church Father qoutes.

Chrysostom:

"And these things are not merely asserted by our own reasoning, but declared to us by the divine oracles, for he himself said, He shall reward everyone according to his works, and not only in hell, but also in the kingdom one will find many differences. For he says, 'In My Father's house are many mansions, and there is one glory for the sun, and another glory for the moon". He declares there is a difference in that world even between one star and another. Knowing then all these things, let us never desist from doing good deeds, nor grow weary, nor, if we shall not be able to reach the rank of the sun or the moon, let us despise that of the stars."

"There is one glory of the sun, another glory of the moon. For as in the earthly bodies there is a difference, so also in the heavenly, and that difference no ordinary one, but reaching to the outer most. There being not only a difference between sun and moon, and stars, but between stars and stars. For what though they all be in heaven? yet some have a larger, others have a lessor share of glory. What do we learn from this? That although they all be in God's kingdom, all shall not enjoy the same reward, and although all sinners may be in hell, they shall not receive the same punishment"

Basil:

"For who is so ignorant of the good thing prepared by God for them that are worthy, as not to know that the crown of righteousness is the graces of the spirit, bestowed in more abundance and perfect measure in that day, when spiritual glory shall be distributed to each in proportion as he shall nobly have played the man? For among the glories of the saints are many mansions in the Father's house, that is difference of dignities, for

as star differs from star in glory, so also is the resurrection of the dead."

Jerome:

"In My Father's house are many mansions, I suppose there are different degrees of merits, One star differs from another star in glory." And in the one body of the Church there are different members. The sun has its own splendour, the moon tempers the darkness of the night, and the five heavenly bodies which are called planets traverse the sky in different tracks and degrees of luminousness. There are countless other stars who moments we trace in the firmament, each has its own brightness."

Origen:

'There is one glory of the sun, and another of the moon, and another of the stars, and star differs from star in glory. Therefore, those who seek for the glory, of the resurrection and for honor and incorruption, shall surely attain to what is written. The body is sown to dishonour, it will rise in glory. It is sown in corruption; it will rise incorruption. So the one who searches for this glory and honor and incorruption through perseverance in good works will attain to eternal life."

Tertullian:

"Those also who after Him are heavenly are understood to have this celestial quality predicated of them not their present nature, but from their future glory, because in a proceeding sentence, which originated this distinction respecting differences of dignity, there was shown to be, one glory of the sun, one glory of the moon, and another glory of the stars, for even one star

differs from another in glory. Then after seeing the difference of worth and dignity, which is even now to be attained at, and then at last to be enjoyed, the apostle adds an exhortation, that we should both here in our training follow the example of Christ, and there attain His eminence of glory. As we have born the image of the earthly, let us also bear the image of the heavenly."[113]

Jesus said, 'My Father's house has many rooms; if that were not so, I would have told you that. I am going there to prepare a place for you? (John 14:2) - In my Father's house are many mansions; or, abiding-places, homes of rest and peace and sojourn in Eden.

"A large house contains not only vessels of gold and silver, but also of wood and clay. Some indeed are for honorable use, but others are for common use. So, if anyone cleanses himself of what is unfit, he will be a vessel for honor; sanctified, useful to the Master, and prepared for every good work." (2 Timothy 2:20)

In these abiding, dwelling places in heaven, there are areas in Eden outside the City that are rather dim of light. The light shines in the City, and the furthest you go from the City, the rays of glory (light) dimmers, and fades[114]. The glory you shine, is

---

[113] I am very thankful to Marty Cauley for his research on finding the above Church Father quotes.
[114] 'You are the light of the world. A city that is set on a hill cannot be hidden.' (Matt 5:14) - 'The city had no need of the sun or of the moon to shine in it, for the glory of God illuminated it. The Lamb is the light.' (Rev 21:23) - 'Send him out to outer darkness' (Matt 22:13). The darkness is from being at a distance from the light of the City in Eden.

the access to the degree of lighted places in heaven you will dwell. You will still able to visit the throne, but your home dwelling may be further away. It matters how you live on earth...[115]

I had the privilege of staying at a children's orphanage in the jungles of India, where young children were having visions of heaven. They have had these encounters now daily for 12 years.

During one of the weeks I was there, the children would come back from their visions (worship/prayer times) and share where Jesus had taken them. This week was unusual, they spoke about Jesus taking them to an area in heaven that was dim, and the light was grey. They said it was not like the rest of heaven, being bright with colour and great light. This place was kind of dark and far from the light of the City. Each day they would come back and share more. One time, they took fruit from the garden to feed the people there. These people weren't in torment, but they weren't that happy. What was this place I kept asking myself.

> *"As the week passed, we learnt that this small area is outside the City, outside of the reach of the light of the City at some distance. The people there, who believers, look skinny with plain clothes, no beautiful garments on like the rest in Heaven. There were a few houses, and they looked like little huts in the forest land. Some people were praising God by the rocks of a stream and others were weeping. You may be thinking, is this place Hell? No, it is in Heaven, and those there are in the kingdom, but have lived extremely carnal and abusive lives as believers."*[116]

---

[115] "There are various abodes according to the worth of those who have believed." (Clement of Alexandria, AD 195)

[116] My personal conversations with those who were involved in receiving this revelation.

Their clothing, their skinny bodies revealed their spiritual maturity and lack of growth in sanctification[117]. This area is a place for carnal believers, gross living, and for those who damage others. They are saved, but they are not prepared or sanctified to a degree to go further. These will stay here until they have untangled soul issues and brought forth healing. It is of my opinion and force from the Scriptures that it does matter how we live on earth.[118]

---

[117] John Bunyan in a vision recalls, 'Some saints shined brighter than others, those who have the most enlarged capacity do love God to the most, and are therefore changed into His likeness. This is the highest glory heaven can give. Nor let this seem strange to you, for even among God's flaming angels there are diversities of order and degrees of glory.' - And, Richard Sigmund, 'I believe that garments were rewards that were being heaped up in heaven. In heaven God rewards us for what we give on earth. Some people were dressed in pants and pull over shirts that were pure white, I also saw people like you would see angels, long flowing robes.'

[118] 'There is a saying among Rabbis in Yalcut Simeoni, page 2, fol. 10, 'The faces of the righteous shall be, in the world to come, like suns, moons, the heavens, stars, lightnings; and like the lilies and candlesticks of the temple.'

CHAPTER 15 - MYSTERY STONES OF SAPPHIRES

PRE-EXISTENCE – THE HIDDEN MYSTERY

In eternity before we existed, God sat on His Sapphire Throne, and before Him was a garden sanctuary[119] seated inside a Rock cave[120]. The sanctuary Temple, was a garden wilderness in darkness. When God decided to bring us forth out of His uncreated light, He placed us deep in the ground (Temple). We came from Him as precious stones, little lights, hidden like a mystery by wisdom in the Temple. As little spirit's, precious stones, we sat there in the dark bathing in the fire of His glory (stones of fire[121]) in the heavenly earth realm. Then God said, let there be light, and there was light, and we were brought up out of the Temple (ground) in the wilderness and stood in the light of God reflecting His light watching the visibility of Paradise appear all around us[122]. The hidden mystery, that being "us" came forth out of the darkness that dwelt around God, and the mist of His presence brought us life and love and fellowship. We heard His booming voice as His love flowed over us.

---

[119] Jeremiah 17:12, "A glorious high throne from the beginning, is the place of our sanctuary".
[120] Cave; - Psalm 27:5, Zephaniah 2:6-7 - Also - In Genesis 28:19, there is a reference to a place called Luz, the place where Jacob had his dream of the heavenly ladder (House of God). The Talmud (B.Sot 53a) identifies this city of Luz as a city of immortals, hidden by an almond tree. The only way into this city was through the inside of the hallow tree trunk through a secret cave which led into the holy land.
[121] The Septuagint translation of Ezekiel 28, refers to the Stones of Fire as the divine abode, throne room.
[122] Genesis 1:3, 'Let there be light', Hebrews 11:3, 'By faith we understand the worlds were framed' - Enoch was shown God speaking to the uncreated light, 'I command in the lowest parts, that visible physical things should come down from the invisible (spiritual) and Adoil came down very great, and I beheld him, and lo! He had a belly of great light, and I said to Him, become undone Adoil, and let the visible come out of you. And he came undone, and a great light came out. And I was in the midst of the great light, and as there is born light from light, there came forth a great age, and showed all creation, which I had thought to create. And I saw that is was good. (Enoch 25:1-4)

"As for the earth, from it comes bread, but underneath it is turned up as by fire. Its stones are the source of sapphires, and it contains gold dust. That path no bird knows, nor has the falcon's eyes seen it. The proud lions have not trodden it, nor has the fierce lion passed over it. He puts his hand on the flint; He overturns the mountains at the roots. He cut channels in the rocks. And his eye sees every precious thing. He dams up the streams from tickling, what is hidden he brings forth to light." (Job 28:6-11)

"My frame was not hidden from You, When I was made in secret, and skilfully wrought in the lowest parts of the earth. Your eyes saw my substance, being yet unformed. And in Your book, they were written, the days fashioned for me. When as yet there were none for me." (Psalm 139:13-16)

The expression; *"lowest parts of the earth"*, is used of the unseen world, the state before birth, the dark void of night. It is also symbolic of the womb, "Sheol, the barren womb - land which is never satisfied" (Prov 30:16)[123]. One by one we came forth like sparks, shimming lights, candle flames.[124]

Each soul is a tread of light, that works together to knit the tapestry of humanity. To be *"wrought"*, is to be embroidered, and this was dedicated for the "art" of the sanctuary. We are a

---

[123] Other references - Ezekiel 31:16, says, 'All that drink water, shall be comforted in the nether parts of the earth', and Psalm 63:10, speaks of the secret laboratory of the earth."

[124] Scripture seems to have more than one fulfilment, as below, first above -"But you are a chosen generation a royal priesthood, a holy nation, His own special people, that you may proclaim the praises of Him who called you out of darkness into his marvelous light." (1 Peter 2:9)

fashioned soul of art, a weaved garment of different colours from God.

Where it says, *"the stones are the source of sapphires, and it contains gold dust"*[125], this is speaking of the transcendent element of man, his soul garment[126], which shines like the sun. The term "dust" is used of a spiritual material instead of the dust of the clay, earthly material.[127]

As for the *"silver cord is broken"* in Ecclesiastes 1:26, this speaks of our earthly appointed times. The word "silver" (Keseph) means an "appointed time", and the word "cord" (Chebel) speaks of our sustained existence. When the cord fades and breaks we die and leave the earth.

The Church Father Arnobius of Sicca, 326 AD, in his work Against Heathens" - wrote,

> *"But let us not reason from things terrestrial as regards things celestial, our coarse material fabrics are "shadows of the true." The robes of light are realities, and are conformed to spiritual bodies, as even here a mist may envelop a tree."*

We came out of the wilderness into His light and God saw our "form" and said, let me hear your voice, for your voice is sweet and your form is lovely.

---

[125] Ian Clayton says, "When the son or daughter of a Hebrew family married a Gentile, after the bride and bridegroom had come out of the huppah, they would take diamond, gold and sapphire dust and throw it over the bride and bridegroom as the power of endowment and their acceptance and sanctification of marriage."
[126] Psalm 8:5, Crowned him with glory and honor, and 2 Enoch 22:9 speaks of Enoch being dressed in the garments of glory. Gold represents glory!
[127] Gold dust, flakes can be made into gold thread. Golds speaks of coming from an incorruptible divine nature - God.

> *"By Wisdom is a house built, by understanding it is made secure, and by knowledge its rooms are filled with all kinds of costly, pleasant possessions." (Proverbs 23:3-4)*

> *"O my dove, in the cleft of the rock in the secret place of the steep pathway. Let me see your 'form', let me hear your voice, for your voice is sweet and your form is lovely." (Song of Solomon 2:14)*

> *"Who is this coming out of the wilderness, like Pillars of smoke, perfumed with myrrh and frankincense..." (Song of Solomon 3:6)*

We were born in heaven in the dark sanctuary, a garden wilderness. As precious stones, God's light shone on us and with His voice and presence betrothed us, and we lived in His glorious light and received our irrevocable callings. The bride-chamber is where we soaked in unity and communion with God's presence. It is where we became entwined with the record of God's DNA.[128]

> *"In Him was DNA, and the DNA was the light of men." (John 1:4)*

In the fire of God's glory, the stones of fire stood, these are the true members of the Temple, it is an altar of stones (souls)

---

[128] As we came forth in God's light, the Hebrew living letters of the DNA of God started to mould us. These letters are called "letters of foundation" or "stones". The Jewish Mishnah uses the phase 'engraved and Hewed (Isa 49:16). To "engrave" is to chisel the letters in stone, sculpturing, while "hewed", means to cut the letters out of the stone the way rock is quarried from a mountain. Once our spirits were formed, sculpted, we were weaved like tapestry with fine details. The letters bringing forth 'form'.

before the throne of God, where souls are engraved, cut, fashioned, betrothed and made perfect in the fire.[129]

It is also where we dance with God (the bridegroom), and shared DNA. The dance is called the *"segullah"*, which means *"treasured possession"*. The dance is worship, it is intimacy, it is where couples breathe their first breaths together. Each moment is pregnant with meaning and beautiful awe.

> *"Let them praise His name with the dance."* (Psalm 149:3)

According to ancient rabbinic tradition the bride-chamber was designed to resemble the sanctuary. It was also Jewish customary for wedding celebrations to last an entire week.[130]

In Genesis 1:27 the heavenly man (us) was created in the image of God, while Genesis 2:7 states that Adam was formed from the dust of the earth. Adam's spirit was sent down from heaven and breathed into his body in the earthly garden temple.[131] For Paradise was above before the throne, and on earth was a garden in Eden, the realms interchanging. The word Paradise comes from the Persian word 'pairidaezas' which means "Walled Garden", there is more than one garden[132]. We came forth as spirit's first in heaven as a reflection of the image of

---

[129] Enoch was taken to the beginning and was shown them in his vision, "Then that angel came to me, and with his voice saluted me, saying, they are the offspring of a man, who are born for righteousness." (1 Enoch 14:17)

[130] Brant Pitre, Jesus the Bridegroom, Image New York Publishers, 2014, p.108

[131] God, with the angels, and created souls (all are a type of Elohim) agreed that a 'figure called man' would be created, and souls would incarnate into 'clay formed beings' on the earth representing the image and likeness of God.

[132] The Talmudic and Midrash sources know of two Gardens of Eden; the terrestrial, of abundant fertility and vegetation, and the celestial, which serves as the habitation of souls of the righteous.

God, out of the Temple (ground), and then after our betrothal covenant and council we were sent to earth into flesh bodies at our appointed times of history...

"According to Midrash ha-Ne'elam, Zohar Haddish 17c, God gathered the dust for Adams' body from the site where the temple in Jerusalem would be built in the future, and drew down his soul from the celestial temple."[133]

"Another interpretation is found in Pirkei-de-Rabbi Eliezer 12, where it is said again, that God took Adam's dust from a pure place, the place of the temple."[134]

In Genesis 2:12, it mentions that there is a river, one of four, and the onyx stone is there in the land. This river came from the throne of God down to the Garden below. The Onyx stones "form" in the spring of water[135] and this is symbolic of us coming down from heaven through the portal of the river. It is also interesting to note, that Jewish tradition says, "that in the wilderness on earth real precious stones fell with the manna around the tabernacle." As in heaven, so on earth, symbolically representing, "us", We came down from heaven. The pattern is there...

The Scholar G. K. Beale says,

"According to Jewish tradition, precious stones fell along with the manna" (cf. Midr. Psalm 78:4)[136]

This Jewish tradition of the stones coming down I document extensively in my book, 'Wilderness Like Eden'.

---

[133] Schwartz, p. 127
[134] p.133
[135] https://stoneandonyx.com/2020/12/17/new-blog-about-stone/
[136] Richard Fellows, Wilderness Like Eden, WordWyze Publishers, 2019, p. 28

In the wilderness God was leading His people, comforting and encouraging His people, His bride to walk with Him. Let our hearts push on for the glorious reunion of the Marriage Supper of the Lamb.

> *"The Nazirites were brighter than snow, and whiter than milk. They were more ruddy in body than rubies, like sapphire in their appearance." (Lamentations 4:7)*

When we came down from heaven, as precious stones of the altar sanctuary into this fallen world, we became dim, our gold garments, our nature like precious stones faded,

> *"How the gold has become dim! How changed the fine gold! The stones of the sanctuary are scattered, At the head of every street. The precious sons of Zion, Valuable as fine gold. How they are regarded as clay pots, the work of the hands of the potter." (Lamentations 4:1-2)*

But we are now being polished and transformed,

> *"Coming to Him as to a living stone, rejected indeed by men, but chosen by God and precious, you also, as living stones, are being built up a spiritual house, a holy priesthood, to offer up spiritual sacrifices acceptable to God through Jesus Christ." (1 Peter 2:4-5)*

CHAPTER 16 - JOB 38:7

The Book of Job, is a very interesting book, and I would like us to reflect on one main verse as we come close to the end of our study, that is Job 38:7. It is debated by many that this Chapter, speaks about pre-existence. Most Evangelical Christians will say it doesn't, and this is mainly due to their understanding of not seeing pre-existence in the Bible. But as we have seen throughout this book, I have made the case for pre-existence. In this reflection I will try and make the case that Job 38:7 is part of that case.

> *"Where were you when I laid the foundations of the earth? Tell Me, if you have understanding. Who determined its measurements? Surely you know! Or what stretched the line upon it? To what were its foundations fastened? Or who laid the cornerstone, When the morning stars sang together, And the sons of God shouted for joy." (Job 38:4-7)*
>
> *"Do you know it, because you were born then, or because the number of your days is great?" (Job 38:21)*

Some are quick to say, "whatever Job 38:7 is about, Job was not there as if he was he would of remembered". But as we have seen the Bible and Jewish Theology says, that we have a veil of forgetfulness over us once in the world (1 Cor 13:12), so Job wouldn't remember. God is pulling Job up because he is complaining about events and the hardship of life, when in true light he knew of these difficult seasons of his life in eternity, but while in the earth realm he is not trusting the steps of the Lord (Psalm 37:23)[137]. We don't always know our path or see each step because it is a journey of faith in a fallen world. God is saying,

---

[137] Psalm 37:23 'The steps of a good man are ordained (established) by the

"stop attacking the season and My Wisdom and trust me". God says, "do you know about the beginning of creation because you were born then."

Who are the Morning Stars? we know that Jesus is the great *'Morning Star'* (God), so if "all" the morning stars sang together, the "term" must have a general meaning[138], as Jesus is not an angel[139]. If we say that the morning stars are angels or other beings[140], 'all', including Jesus, at the revealing of creation would have been early lights in the morning, as the dawn[141] of creation came into being and visibility appeared from darkness. Jesus came out of the Father as the light of the world, and shone upon the darkness, and all the morning stars were seen clearer as the darkness became light like the morning dawn. If the morning stars sang together, who are the sons of God who shouted for joy? These sons bear likeness to God, as holy, spirits, that honour and obey him.

Jesus inaugurates in the heavens the daylight portion of the *'Day of the Lord'*. The night-time portion will be the darkness that precedes, since the biblical "day" officially starts at night-time. There was the day of the Lord at the start of creation, and there will be also the day of the Lord when He returns. Peter says, "that this "Morning Star" will rise in our hearts (2 Peter

---

Lord, and he delight in his way'. And - 'Though he slay me, yet will I trust in him: but I will maintain mine own ways before him.' (Job 13:15).

[138] Angels are called Morning Stars, and also Jesus is, but although his name is similar, he is the Great (Bright) Morning Star. Jesus as the light of the world is the true light of which the others reflect.

[139] But he takes the name in Genesis 16:7-13 as the Angel of the Lord who is Yahweh.

[140] Lucifer was a Morning Star. Translations of Isaiah 14:12 seem to vary a lot: Lucifer, son of the morning, son of the dawn, star of the morning, morning star, day star. The name "Lucifer" means harbinger (or messenger) of light. Is Job 38:7 talking about one group or two groups of beings?

[141] All would have been early lights, but Jesus was the True light that was the light of dawn lighting up the rest.

1:19), He is referring to the time when we will see the future daylight part; of the Day of the Lord. To muddle the waters a bit, is it possible to say that maybe anyone who was there at creation was a morning star.[142] As Jesus shines through us and we are members of his body, He will rise in our hearts. Could we in fact be part of the morning stars, a general term for "spiritual beings"[143].

Comparing and relating humans to angels was in the time of the Apostle Paul an important feature of Jewish life[144]. We must also remember there are different types of elohim, in Job 38;7, and stars, of the house-hold of God, so could it be talking about all types.[145]

> *"And so we have a prophetic word confirmed, which you do well to heed as a light dawns and the morning star rises in your heart." (2 Peter 1:19)*

For the sake of it, we will at this stage say, the morning stars are angels and the sons of God are humans (but it could very well be the other option that it is talking of both)[146]. It could also be that the two terms, morning stars and sons of God are a flow of words speaking of the same being. Let's see where our study goes…

---

[142] 2 Peter 1:18, 'And we heard this voice which came from Heaven when we were on the Mountain.'.

[143] Interesting to note, the Biblical name Ester refers to the name Venus (star). Venus is known as the Morning Star. The ancients commonly described the planets as 'wondering stars' (Jude 1:13)

[144] Guy Williams, The Spirit World in the letters of Paul the Apostle; A Critical Examination of the Role of Spiritual Beings in the Authentic Pauline Epistles.

[145] Michael S. Heiser, The Unseen Realm, Lexham Press, 2015, p.32.

[146] Not that I promote Mormonism; but they have an interesting interpretation, 'Some men are "Morning Stars" of the first magnitude, possessing, a luminescence so unique, so compelling, that lesser mortals bask in their reflected glory like so many planets orbiting the sun." (D&C 88:40)

Abram was told to looked up at the sky and count the descendants of heaven as the stars of the sky (Genesis 15:5).[147]

In Genesis 37:9, Joseph has a dream where he sees the sons of Jacob as stars. Second Temple thought, including, 'Philo of Alexandria' held to a kind of angelification (glorification) of believers. We even see this in Mark 12:35, which says, 'in the resurrection we will be like (similar) the angels.

The Jewish text of 2 Bar. 51:10, says that, "they will live in the heights of the world and they will be like the angels and be equal to the stars."

The morning star is a symbol of the ancestors in Native American cultures. They link the symbolism of the star to their elders, past spirits, and ancestors.

2 Enoch 30:12, even describes Adam as an angel,

> *"I created man from inviable (spiritual) and from (physical) nature, of both are his death and life and image, he knows speech like some created thing, small in greatness and again great in smallness, and I placed him on earth, a second angel, honorable, great and glorious, and I appointed him as ruler to rule on earth and to have wisdom, and there was none like him on earth of all my existing creatures." (2 Enoch 30:12)*

Now, one must understand what I am saying. There is the eternal God (Trinity), then lower elohim (angels), then lower again elohim (humans). Both angels and humans are a type of

---

[147] 'And *they* that be wise, *shall shine*, as the brightness of the firmament: and *they* that turn many to righteousness, *shall shine as the stars*, forever and ever.' (Daniel 12:3) And speaking of us - 'One star differs from another in glory'. (1 Cor 14:41)

elohim, and an elohim is one who has celestial flesh[148]. Elohim as finite ones, basically means, a 'spiritual being' of different ranks, celestial flesh, angelic kind, or godlike ones. The angels are an elder race to us, but we are different to them. There are sub-groups of elohim, for we are family, Jesus even calls us brothers, not because we are eternal or a hundred percent the same, but due to being family.[149]

The Church Father Methodius said, on keeping the distinctions, and differences,

> *"The moon shines like the sun, does not mean that the moon is, in regards, similar to the sun, so the likeness offers only partial parallel."*[150]

The Church Father Origen, said of angels,

> *"We know that angels are superior to men; so that men, when made perfect, become like the angels".*[151]

> *"Scripture admonishes our souls to contemplate the stable nature of the angels, so that our stability in virtue will be fortified by their example. For since it has been promised us that the life after the resurrection will resemble the condition of angels, it follows that our life*

---

[148] Like the angels, Matthew 22:30, Mark 12:55, have celestial flesh 1 Cor 15:35-49 - and 1 John 3:1-3 says, we are holy ones, the same term for angels in the Old Testament. Angels do look similar to humans.

[149] When it comes to Jesus & Lucifer, Jesus is not Lucifer's spirit equal brother. Jesus is eternal, and the Bright Morning Star, the light of the world, and Lucifer is just a created Morning Star. The Mormon Jesus is not the Jesus of the Bible. For them Jesus was not God who became a man, but he was a man who had to prove himself in a mortal body in order to become a 'god'.

[150] Discourse on Resurrection.

[151] Origen, Against Celsus, 4;544-45

in this world should be in conformity with that which will follow."[152]

Biblical Scholar, Michael Bird, in the book, "How God Became Jesus", connects this angel thought to the NT Scriptures,

> *"There is some traction to this view in Christian sources. First consider Acts 12, where Peter escapes from prison, goes to the house of Mary, the mother of John Mark, and knocks on the door. Rhoda hears Peters voice, runs back, and tells the others that it is Peter, and they infer that "it must be his angel" (Acts 12:13-16). In other words, they think that Peter is already dead and the dude at the door must be his angelic body."*[153]

The great Reformed Theologian, B. B. Warfield cites, "Acts of Paul and Theola" a text that dates to the second century as saying, "Blessed are they that fear God, for they shall become angels of God."[154]

"Who are the sons of God, not by birth, as Christ, nor adoption, as saints, but by creation as Adam." (Luke 3:38). Not from human birth, not in the absolute manner like Christ, and not as an adopted saint (a part of sonship), but by creation, Adam. Luke 3:38 calls Adam a Son of God, and we know that all of Adam's descendants were created in the immortal land.[155] 1 Enoch 62:7-

---

[152] Ibid, 4.29, 4;5 09
[153] Michael Bird, How God became Jesus, Zondervan Publishing, 2014, p.36
[154] B. B. Warfield, 'The Angels of Christs Little Ones', In selceted shorter writtings.
[155] Chapter Seven, The Evidence Speaks ; demonstrates this claim.

8 - describes the Son of Man together with the congregation of the Elect before their sowing in the earth[156]. Adam was called a Son of God because he was created directly from God and chosen.[157]

As we saw in Chapter Fifteen, the *'Mystery Sapphire Stones'*; the Garden sanctuary was in darkness until Jesus shone the light of world into it, and then the precious stones came up out of the Temple as sons of God. The morning stars were at the foundation of creation, but they also sang at the creation of our births in heaven as spirits. We all sang and praised experiencing the dawn of our existence in creation.

The morning stars were singing over our births[158], and as in heaven, this is done on earth. They even sang praises at the coming birth of Jesus (Luke 2:13). Even Abraham shouted for joy that he had seen Jesus' day (John 8:56)

Speaking of the angels singing over men,

> *"Praise ye him, sun and moon, praise him, all you stars of light." (Psalm 148:3)*

The sons of God when they came out of the heavenly sanctuary (Temple) into the light of dawn shouted for joy. We see this pattern in Ezra 3:10, and also remember that we are the spiritual temple being built up, the holy priesthood (1 Peter 2:5).

---

[156] 1 Enoch 70:4 says, He saw the fathers of the righteous who from the beginning dwelt in that place.
[157] Elijah was taken directly into Heaven, and also Enoch, could they be considered a Son of God?
[158] The Morning Stars if angels were singing over our births in eternity, but if we are part of the 'term' Morning Stars, then 'all' were singing and praising at each other's existence in the light.

"And when the builders laid the foundation of the temple of the Lord, they set the priest in the apparel with trumpets, and the Levites the sons of Asaph with symbols to praise the Lord, offer ordnances of David king of Israel." (Ezra 3:10)

Robert Alter says in his book, The Wisdom Books, Job, Proverbs, and Ecclesiastes,

"When the morning stars sang, the verb for 'singing' 'ron' is from the same root as renunah 'glad song' which Job (3:7) wished to expunge from the night he was conceived. The morning stars are also a counterpoint to the stars of dawn on the night of the conception that Job wished never to have happened."[159]

"When the morning stars sang together, and all the sons of God shouted for joy? Or who shut up the sea with doors, **when it brake forth, as if it had issued out of the womb?** *When I made the cloud the garment thereof, and thick darkness* **a swaddling band for it"** *(Job 38:7-9).*

The Garden sanctuary above was a like a woman, a garden sealed up until creation. The Garden sanctuary was like a womb[160]. Creation came out into visibility out of the darkness,

---

[159] Robert Altar, *The Wisdom Books, Job, Proverbs, and Ecclesiastes*, Norton & Company; Reprint edition, 2010

[160] "Your people shall be volunteers in the day of Your power. In the beauties of holiness, from the womb of the morning, You have dew of Your youth." (Psalm 110.3)

and not only was the foundation of creation revealed out of the light, but we came forth shouting.[161]

> *"LORD, thou hast been our dwelling place in all generations. Before the mountains were **brought forth**, or ever thou hadst **formed** the earth and the world, even from everlasting to everlasting, thou art God." (Psalm 90:1-2).*

Adam was a Son of God, and also all his dependents in heaven. In the mystery, when they are sent to earth to be born into the earth to be tested by faith, they are to unravel the mystery of who they are, that is our calling manifested. They were to reveal that they are the manifold sons of God, who's journey will be completed when they return to heaven.

Ancient Monotheism and Intermediately Figures

Jewish monotheism has a great awareness that there are many created intermediately figures under God. There are examples of early Jewish texts that describe Adam, Moses, Jacob, Elijah and Enoch (Metratron) as angels. Enoch, in the 'Book of Enoch', is translated into Metratron and is called the lesser YHWH. But these Heavenly beings do not have absolute divine power in the texts. They are appointed agents who work under God and are not worshipped.[162]

---

[161] Why did David dance before the Ark? and why did John leap with joy in his mothers womb? It was because it symbolized "us" when we came forth out of God and danced and leapt for joy in the dawn of the morning of creation before the mercy seat throne of God in Eternity. (2 Sam 6:14 & Luke 1:41).
[162] p.32

> *"For the earnest expectation of the creations eagerly waits for the revealing of the sons of God." (Romans 8:19)*

Jesus says in Revelation 2:28, "To him who overcomes, I will give him the morning star'. This is the right to joint rule with Him."

As we come to the close of this Chapter, I leave the words of Psalm 110:3 to enlighten our hearts.

> *"Your people shall be volunteers (troops) in the day of Your power. In the beauties of holiness, from the womb of the morning, You have dew of Your youth." (Psalm 110.3)*

The passage tells us that the Messiah (eternal Son, King) has dew of His youth. The dew comes from the birth of the morning (dawn) in the beauties of holiness. The dew is God's off-spring, we are His off-spring (Acts 17:28), His people, the members of His Church (Heb 12:23)[163]. These are those who came forth at the dawn of creation. They will be priests of warfare for God, His troops who were chosen and enlisted for sonship (registered) (Heb 12:23).

"You therefore must endure hardship as a good soldier of Jesus Christ. No one engaged in warfare entangles himself with the affairs of this life, that he may please him who enlisted him as a solider." (2 Timothy 2:3-4)

---

[163] The dew of God? In Zohar 3:128a, Idra Rabbah, this dew is described as "the light of the pale glow of the ancient One. And from that dew exists the supernatural saints."

> *"And so we have a prophetic word confirmed, which you do well to heed as a light dawns and the morning star rises in your heart." (2 Peter 1:19).*

> *"However, do not rejoice that the spirits submit to you, but rejoice that your names are written in heaven!" (Luke 10;20).*

As we come to the end of this Chapter, I recommend that we are carefully to not say what I 'am not promoting. I am not saying we are created angels (exactly like the elder race). What I am saying is that the "terms" elohim and angel, are wider terms used in Scripture. We have God being the angel of the Lord, the angel of His presence, and even in Jewish tradition the Holy Spirit was known as an independent angel/messenger who existed eternally before creation[164]. These terms speak of spiritual beings. We must step carefully with our words and definitions.

Biblical Scholar, Michael Heiser says, 'While it is clear that the sons of God were with God before creation, there's a lot about them that isn't clear. In the Hebrew Bible, the sons of God are actually never called angels. That is, there are no passages in which *'beney elohim'* (and similar phases) occur in parallel with *mal'akim* (angels). Later Jewish texts, such as the Septuagint, the Greek translation of the Hebrew Bible, in some instances rendered *beney elohim* as *angeloi* (angels), but such translation decisions are not driven by distinctive Hebrew vocabulary.[165]

---

[164] Dr. Dinah Dye, D Min in Hebraic Studies in Christianity says, 'In Jewish tradition, the Holy Spirit was an independent angel who existed before creation and was co-creator with God.' p.142.
[165] Heiser, p. 24

Speaking of the 'Morning Stars'(Job 38:7), Heiser, says, 'We might think of them as angels, but that wouldn't be quite correct.'[166]

The Jewish 'Thanksgiving Scroll', which was one of the first seven Dead Sea scrolls discovered in 1947, says, 'When the morning stars rejoice together, then all the sons of God shout for joy.' In the scroll the morning stars are alluding to Job 38:7, which the Scroll identifies as Israel (humans/souls).[167]

Peter Schafer, says in his Book, 'Origins of Jewish Mysticism',

> *'In the Thanksgiving Scroll, those who are united in rejoicing are angels and humans, and the only parallel which applies Job 38:7 not just to angels but to both angels and humans is a large midrash complex in the rabbinic literature. There, the "morning stars" are identified with Israel.'*[168]

A morning star is one who has shined in the light of creation. A created elohim, god, angel, one who has celestial flesh. Human spirits were morning stars, created elohim's, and had celestial flesh. Angels also were at the dawn of creation, and also take on the names, morning stars, sons of god, sons of heaven. The term 'morning star' is not one or the other, although human spirits and angels are different. If you were brought forth by God, created in his likeness, you are a morning star, and a son or daughter of God.

---

[166] Heiser, p. 23
[167] I would conclude that the term 'Morning Star" speaks of Spiritual beings - Angels & Human Spirit beings (gods). And Jesus the Eternal Son - is the Great Morning Star.
[168] Peter Shcfer, Origins of Jewish Mysticism, Princeton University Press; 1st edition (2011), p 40.

* Scripture calls us stars,

* Scripture says, the morning star will rise in our hearts - we will be glorified, Christ revealing us.

* The Qumran, Dead Sea Text, claim's we are morning stars, joined/united with the angels shouting,

* Other Rabbinical literature claim we are morning stars,

* Other cultures claim the stars are their elders and descendants,

* Biblical scholars claim the term 'morning stars', is not just identical to calling them angels,

* Conclusion, we are part of the morning stars (Job 38:7).

CHAPTER 17 - GATHERING THOUGHTS

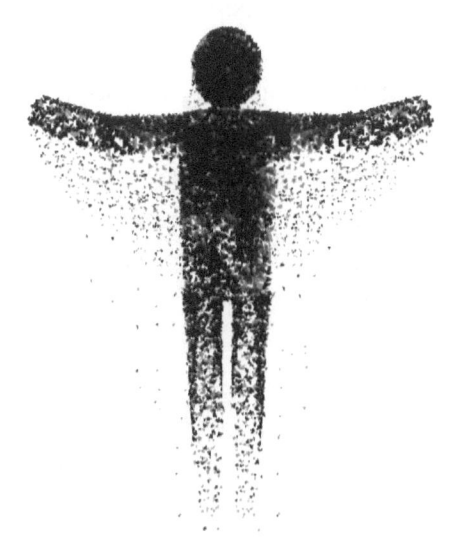

As we come to the last few pages of this book, I will make some concluding remarks. We have been on a journey tracing our existence back into eternity. Through sixteen of the Chapters, I have tried to layout a step-by-step case to demonstrate that we came out of the secret place shining as the hidden mystery. The hidden precious stones, the bride and glorious Church of Eden through the manifold wisdom of God.

I have used extensively Scripture, Commentaries, Jewish Commentaries, Jewish ancient literature, Extra biblical books, and the reflections of the early Church Fathers, and modern Theologians and writers. When I have dealt with the Scriptures in the New Testament, I have stuck with comments and commentaries that are considered Orthodox (Christian). Some may say, I have taken Mormon concepts, but this is incorrect. In two of the Chapters, I analysis the similarities and what makes them different. I show that their concept of God, the Mormon understanding is wrong, and that the idea of deification can be traced back to the biblical Canon of Scripture, and also the early Church Fathers. Mormons believe that God was once a man floating in the Universe, the Father was like a child, and as a man he became God, this I totally reject.

I quote them,

> *"As man is, God once was; as God is, man may become" (Prophet Lorenzo Snow, quoted in Milton R. Hunter, The Gospel Through the ages, 105-106)*[169]
>
> *"Remember that God, our heavenly Father, was perhaps a child, and a mortal like we ourselves, and rose step by step in the scale of progress, in the school of advancement; has moved forward and overcome, until*

---

[169] Walter Martin, The Kingdom of the Cults, Bethany House, 20003, p. 236

He has arrived at the point where He now is" (Apostle Orson Hyde, Journal of Discourse, 1;123.)[170]

The idea of the divine councils is throughout the Old Testament, and mentioned in Jewish Theology.

The doctrine of "Theosis" has a strong appearance in the writings of the early Church Fathers.

> *Methodius, cites Ps. 82:6a (LXX 81:6a) to teach that God grants the title of "gods" to those who are not fleshly but spiritual (De sanguisuga 9.2).*
>
> *Pseudo-Hyppolytus, citations from Ps. 82:6 (LXX 81:6) state, that God had originally made humanity with the aim to become "gods," that is, immortal and incorruptible.*
>
> *Theophilus of Antioch, in the middle of the second century (Autol. 2.27), also taught that humanity was made to become "gods" through maturing to perfection (Autol. 2.24).*

I have also shown that pre-existence is flooded extensively in the early Jewish literature. It is also hinted in a number of biblical Scriptures.

In our lives, let us take the time to reflect that we were in the Garden sanctuary before the throne in heaven. That God knows us personally and has betrothed us in His love. In the hard times, remember that we stood in the council, and the Lord appointed our days, and would of said to our faces - "I will never leave you

---

[170] Martin, p. 236

or forsake you", because you are My bride'. God sent us to earth to reveal the hidden mystery, that we would reveal His image of love and goodness, and justice over evil, as we walk in a dim world, in faithfulness and righteousness to be the light of the world. Let us prepare our heart's and make ourselves ready for the Marriage Supper of the Lamb.

> *"Let us be glad and rejoice, and give honor to him; for the marriage of the Lamb is come, and his wife hath made herself ready." Concerning the wife of the Lamb, John continued to write, "And to her was granted that she should be arrayed in fine linen, clean and white; for the fine linen is the righteousness's of the saints. And he said unto me, Write, Blessed are they who are called unto the marriage supper of the Lamb" (Revelation 19:1-7)*

We are told His wife, bride, made herself ready and that was through the righteous acts of the Saints. It does matter how we live while in this earthly tent we call our bodies, the Temple of God, that houses the image of God.

Many of the early Church Fathers saw this too, that we must prepared our hearts and walk in righteousness and put on the garments.

Irenaeus (180 AD),

> *"He also made it clear that, after our calling, we should be adorned with the works of righteousness, so that the Spirit of God may rest upon us. For this is the wedding garment."*[171]

---

[171] David W. Bercot, A Dictionary of Early Christian Beliefs, Hendrickson Publishers, 1998, p.494

Tertullian (210 AD),

> "Even in the gospel, the wedding garment may be regarded as the sanctity of the flesh."[172]

> "The person who is not clothed at the marriage feast in the garment of good works will have to be bound hand and foot."[173]

Clement of Alexandria (195 AD),

> "It is here that the preparation for entrance to the marriage to which we are invited must be accomplished. The person who has been made ready to enter will say, "My joy is now fulfilled. However, the unadorned and unsightly person will hear, "Friend, how did you come in here without having a wedding garment."[174]

The oil necessary to enter the wedding in Matthew 25:9-10 is bought. The white garments are also bought according to Revelation 3:1. Being dressed in these white garments is to be dressed in the imparted righteousness of readiness and sanctification (Luke 12:35), not merely the imputed righteousness of justification. The urge to buy such clothing is addressed to Christians as something they need to do. If Christians buy clothing, walk in righteous works, open the door of their hearts and keep close fellowship with God, and overcome, they will be

---

[172] p. 494
[173] p. 494
[174] p.494

clothed with white garments, eat with Jesus, and rule with Jesus.[175]

Let us press on toward the goal for the prize of the upward call of God in Christ Jesus. (Philippians 3:14)

> *"The good news of the inexhaustible riches of Christ, and to bring to light what the arrangement of the secret that for the ages was hidden by God, the creator of all things is like. This was so that God's many-sided wisdom might now be made known by the Church to the rulers, and to the authorities, in the heavenly places in agreement with the eternal purpose that He accomplished through Christ Jesus our Lord." (Ephesians 3:8-11)*

Our true purpose is to reflect God's image, and become the "One Man" (Eph 2:15), that walks through creation (all members), and the universe being the grand demonstration to all that exists.

---

[175] Marty Cauley, The Outer Darkness, Misthological Press, 2012, p. 565

CHAPTER 18 - WOMB OF GOD

"Clouds and darkness surround Him, righteousness and justice are the foundation of His throne." (Psalm 97:2)[176]

"The earth was without form, and void and darkness was on the face of the deep." (Genesis 1:2)[177]

"The grave, the barren womb, the earth that is not satisfied with water, and the fire never says enough." (Proverbs 30:16).

"A garden enclosed, is my sister, my spouse, a spring shut up, a fountain sealed." (Song of Songs 4:12).

"And the Spirit of God was hovering over the face of the waters." (Genesis 1:2).[178]

"Or who shut in the sea with doors, when it burst forth and issued from the womb." (Job 38:8).[179]

"O, my dove in the clefts of the rock, in the secret places of the cliff, (Song of Songs 2;14).[180]

"Then God said, Let there be light and there was light." (Genesis 1:3).[181]

---

[176] In the beginning there was just God who dwelt in darkness.
[177] The earth was without form and void, it was like a wasteland or wilderness in darkness. It was like a cave in the earth, a womb. (Genesis 1: 2 and Proverbs 30:16).
[178] And the Spirit of God was hovering over the Garden Sanctuary, breathing and vibrating over the entrance of the forest cliff opening.
[179] The Garden's spring was sealed, it's fountain (Song of Song 4:12), and as God hovered, breathed, vibrated over (Genesis 1:2) it, it became aroused and started to drip and then burst forth from deep within the womb (Garden/Vagina/Temple/Sanctuary) through the sealed doors.
[180] A cleft in the Rock is a narrow opening to a secret place deep inside the Garden womb of God.
[181] Then God said, Let there be light and there was light, the eternal Son came forth as the light of the world, and conceived and birthed seed deep in the womb.

"Your people shall be troops in the day of Your power, in the beauties of holiness, from the womb of the morning, You have the dew of Your youth." (Psalm 110:3)[182]

"A glorious high throne from the beginning is the place of our sanctuary" (Jeremiah 17:12)

"Listen to me, you who follow after righteousness. You who seek the Lord; Look to the rock from which you were hewn, and to the hole of the pit from which you were dug." (Isaiah 51:1)[183]

"Its stones are the source of sapphires and it contains gold dust. That path no bird knows, nor has the falcons eye seen it. The proud lions have not trodden it, nor has the fierce lion passed over it. He puts his hand on the flint, He overturns the mountains at the roots, He cuts out channels in the rocks, and his eyes sees every precious thing. What is hidden he brings to light.' (Job 28:6-11)

"My frame was not hidden from You, when I was made in secret, and skilfully wrought in the lowest parts of the earth." (Psalm 139:15).[184]

"The Lord possessed me at the beginning of His way, before His works of old. I have been established from everlasting, from the beginning, before there was ever an earth ... Then I was be-

---

[182] God's children were conceived in the light, in the womb of the dawn, in beauty and holiness (Psalm 110:3).

[183] Temples in the Ancient Near East were generally constructed from stone blocks. Aven, the Hebrew word for stone, is formed from two words; Av (father) and ben (son). Ben also comes from the root word 'banah' which means to build. The Father through the Son, brought forth the mystery and built the spiritual house from precious stones, for which we are (1 Peter 2:5).

[184] All God's children came forth in the light, we came out of the rock (Christ), out of the earth temple as precious stones and we were engraved, weaved and knitted together as spirit beings. We were made in the lowest parts of the earth, the netherworld, other-word above, but under God's throne in the cave of His womb drawn up before the altar.

side Him as a master craftsman, and I was daily His delight, rejoicing always before Him, rejoicing in His inhabited world, and my delight was the sons of men." (Proverbs 8:22, 23, 30, 31)[185]

"You show that you are a letter from Christ, the result of our ministry, written not with ink but with the Spirit of the living God" (2 Corinthians 3:3)[186]

"For in Him we lived and moved and had our being, for we are His offspring" (Acts 17:28).

"He who dwells in the secret place of the Most High, shall abide under the shadow of the Almighty. I will say of the Lord, He is my refuge and my fortress, My God, in Him I will trust." (Psalm 91:1-2)

"Just as He chose us in Him before the foundation of the world, that we should be holy and without blame before Him in love." (Ephesians 1:4)[187]

"Let me see your 'form', let me hear your voice, for your voice is sweet and your form is lovely." (Song of Songs 2:14).

"Before I formed you in the womb I knew you, before you were born, I sanctified you, I ordained you a prophet to the nations." (Jeremiah 1:5)[188]

---

[185] The Spirit of Wisdom from eternity, as a master craftsman, She weaved, made our spirits like a tapestry.

[186] The living letters that formed us in Heaven have made us a revealing letter (of many words) in the earth. Our spirits are the treasure that is hidden in earthen vessels (2 Cor 4:7).

[187] We came forth and lived, moved and had our being in Him in eternity, He saw our form and beauty in the womb of the dawn. We were chosen in Him to be blameless in love.

[188] Before Jeremiah was born in his mother's womb, God knew him intimately, and set him apart and ordained him to be a Prophet.

"Your eyes saw my substance, being yet unformed, and in Your book they all were written the days fashioned for me, when as yet there were none of them." (Psalm 139:16)[189]

"Of the Rock who begot you, you are unmindful, and have forgotten the God who gave birth to you." (Deuteronomy 32:18)

"I have held My peace a long time, I have been still and restrained Myself. Now I will cry like a woman in Labour. I will pant and gasp at once." (Isaiah 42:14).[190]

"In Him also we have obtained an inheritance, being predestined according to the purpose of Him who works all things according to the council of His will." (Ephesians 1:11).[191]

"Have the gates of death been revealed to you? Or have you seen the doors of the shadow of death?" (Job 38:17)[192]

Every good gift and every perfect gift is from above, and comes down from the Father of lights, with whom there is no variation or shadow of turning. Of His own will He brought us forth by the word of Truth..." (James 1:17)[193]

---

[189] God saw our substance, our spirits, before we were formed in the earth with earthly bodies. He wrote our days before we had lived one of them on earth. We must remember there is a Heaven earth, Eden, and an earthly earth, planet earth.

[190] God reminds us that we were begot from the Rock and He gave birth to us and He gave Labour to us.

[191] At our appointed times, we are sent to the earth (Acts 17:26), we are predestined with a mission and purpose, an inheritance, worked out by God in His council. Then we were touched on the face by the angel of conception and our memories of Heaven faded and we were sent into our mothers' wombs to see dimly once born.

[192] These are the portals out of Heaven and into the world.

[193] Every perfect gift, every perfect spirit, like a little candle comes down from the Father of lights.

"And it happened, when Elizabeth heard the greeting of Mary, that the babe leaped in her womb, and Elizabeth was filled with the Holy Spirit." (Luke 1:41)

"For he will be great in the sight of the Lord, and shall drink neither wine nor strong drink. He will also be filled with the Holy Spirit, even from his mother's womb." (Luke 1:15)

"Can a woman forget her nursing child, and not have compassion on the son of her womb, surely they may forget. Yet, I will not forget you. see, I have engraved you on the palms of my hands, your walls are continually before Me.' (Isaiah 49:15-16)

The Hebrew word for 'mercy' (re-chem) is related to the word for womb. To live within God's compassion is to rest within God's womb.

In the Zohar[194], there is the feminine image of God, called Binah (Understanding), also known as 'Immah Ilaah' (the higher Mother) who is called the womb, and palace of creation[195], the foundation of understanding, the well of souls. The womb is the quarry that is carved out by the light of the Wisdom of God. It is the treasury of wisdom, the quarry where God hewed out, by the living letters of the Spirit our existence. God's spirit was engraving by casting the letters to weave and thread our 'form' into existence (in the secret place of the cliff, let me see your form - Song of Songs 2:14).

The letters weaved like golden tread in a dance of light, and knitted our individual spirits clothing together. This tapestry of our spiritual DNA vibrates and sings a song to God as He sings

---

[194] I quote the Zohar, because what it describes is in the Biblical Scriptures.
[195] Christian Mystic, Teresa de Avila also grasped the knowledge of the palace of creation, in her work called, 'Interior Castle'. In many cultures the word palace, castle, mansion or house refer to the womb of creation.

us into existence. We are a song to the Lord that vibrates a frequency like a hologram of God's image, but with our own individual code[196].

> *"The royal daughter is all glorious within the palace, her clothing is woven with gold. She shall be brought to the King in robes of many colours." (Psalm 45:13)*

> *"Behold, God is my salvation, I will trust and not be afraid. For Yah, the Lord, is my strength and song." (Isaiah 12:2)*

This place of our making is the womb of God, it is the blueprint of our original innocence, our true identity.

When all the children of the mystery had come forth, they stood in the Womb, Palace, Temple, Enclosed Garden, City Bride. They stood before the throne and fountain of living water, the water of life. The living water that holds the code of life is like a drink when we come to earth to restore health and infuse the soul with liquid light. When we bath and drink the water of life it realigns our DNA to its original state.[197]

---

[196] DNA has a sound, vibration, song. African tribes know of the 'song of the soul'. The custom says, that the mother can hear the song of their spirit baby. The father and mother then learn the song together and when they make love, they sing the song together and invite the child in. They invite the weaved child to come into conception. Science has also discovered that our DNA has a sound and frequency. When God weaved us together, the threads were weaved to sing through a dance, our souls' existence. Even spider webs have been shown at the University of Oxford to transmit a song of information.

[197] Also, in Heaven there is a fountain of Jesus' blood, and in the blood there is life. This blood is like the placenta in the womb. A child in the womb eats and drinks the body and blood of its mother. Jesus said, unless you eat His body and drink His blood you would not have life. In the womb there is union, two become one. If one is joined to the Lord, they are one in spirit, weaved in union.

Jesus said, if you drink this water, a fountain of eternal life will flow within your belly, your womb (John 7:38:39). The water holds the memory of creation out of the Spirit of Wisdom.

The act of love, covenant sex, between a man and woman is to weave and entangle together and become one as co-creators. We are to image God's conception and the womb as it is in heaven. It is so important that a child is brought into earthly existence through the union of true love. Love imprints its message, frequency, into the child's make up. Once a child is conceived, the environment shapes it's biological and emotionally states. The environment can make the child have an orphan spirit before they are even born. Our experiences shape our epigenetic modification of our DNA. A child's soul enters the womb with it own individual DNA blueprint, but it is also weaved together from the record and vibrations of its parents, positive or negative inheriting traits. The state of their song can tarnish the song of the child.

Azra Bertrand says, in a perfect world,

> *"In original innocence you would have been conceived in the immaculate conception of sacred union, gestated in a Holy Womb clear from any negative physical imprints, energetic, psychic, and spiritual imprints; your genetic inheritance would be selected from a banquet of the finest jewels of your lineage, and you would enter this realm birthed in ecstatic, orgasmic waves of pure love. You would be born through love, gestated and genetically coded to receive love. You would be a being of love, and earth would be your paradise."*[198]

---

[198] Azra Bertrand, Womb Awakening, Initiatory Wisdom from the Creatrix of All Life, Kindle 2017, p.228.

When a mother and father are connected in love, in a loving relationship, the baby is flooded with the hormones and neurotransmitters of bliss, which pass through the placenta immediately to the baby, which become wired into the baby to receive joy. In the journey of pregnancy everything matters to the formation of the child in the womb, our words, actions, thoughts, and prayers.[199]

> *"Finally, brothers, whatever is true, whatever is noble, whatever is right, whatever is pure, whatever is lovely, whatever is admirable - if anything is excellent or praiseworthy think about such things. Whatever you have learned or received or heard from me, or seen in me, put into practice. And the peace of God will be with you." (Philippians 4:8)*

The existence of our soul is like a weaved tapestry. We are God's workmanship created for good works. We were weaved in the womb of God and sent down into the weaving of our parents, being knitted in the womb of the tent of our mothers. Then born into the tent, tabernacle of creation, into the tapestry of history. Our individual bodies are also a tabernacle of which our soul is to weave a beautiful expression of love throughout life. Surrendering and weaving into the nature of God, with gold, blue, purple and scarlet thread to produce glorious garments.[200]

> *"Of the blue, purple, and scarlet thread they made garments of ministry, for ministering in the holy place...*

---

[199] In Cyndi Dales book, The Subtle Body, she says, 'DNA is a storage unit of light and a source of biophoton emission. Dr. Leonard Herowitz has shown that DNA emits and receives phonons and photons, the electromagnetic waves of sound and light. DNA interacts with light and our thoughts, prayers and intentions have also been shown to affect DNA. - Proverbs 17:22, p.45.

[200] At the end of our journey on earth, when we live in heaven, our garments and colours will speak individually of our works and our transformation in holiness.

> *And beat the gold into thin sheets and cut it into threads, to work it in with blue, purple, and scarlet thread, and the fine linen, into artistic designs." (Exodus 39:1,3)*

> *"But He knows the way that I take, when He has tested me, I shall come forth as gold." (Job 23:10)*

The whole journey, the mystery has already been written on the timeline before the throne, for God knows the beginning and the end.[201]

> *"For whom He foreknew, He also predestined to be conformed to the image of His Son, that He might be the firstborn among many brethren. Moreover, whom He predestined, these He also called; whom He called, these He also justified; and whom He justified, these He also glorified." (Romans 9:29-30)*

---

[201] Midrash Rabbah Exodus 35:6; Midrash Rabbah Numbers 4:13; Midrash Song of Songs 3:10, 3 Enoch 45, describe the curtain before the Holy One, as having printed on it all the events throughout world history.

CHAPTER 19 - INTERPRETATIONS

In my interpretation of the book of Song of Solomon, some may find that they need more insights to see the connections I have drawn. The book has many layers of revelation and some may not have seen my interpretation before, so I add this Chapter to help.

The book of Song of Solomon has been interpreted in the following ways,

* A love story between Solomon and the Shulamite woman.

* A love story between Christ and His Church - the mystery of marriage is to show Christ's love for His Church.

* God's love towards a believer's soul.

* A picture of God and the immaculate conception through Mary.

* The Kabbalistic Shiur Qomah, describing the groom's body as God's own form or face.

* The Zohar, describing a dialogue between the feminine and masculine aspects of divinity.

* Early Syriac Churches believed that God was the groom.

* God's love for Creation and His People in a betrothal Covenant.

Whichever interpretation you take, there are intimate, graphic details, that one must all interpret. It would be easy to follow the interpretation of Solomon and the Shulamite woman, a basic love scene, but I believe that the text says so much more. My interpretation is to look for a deeper spiritual significance behind the text. It is more spiritual, than literal I believe, or as Augustine writes, "It is a rapture veiled in allegory."

Some of the Church Fathers that taught the book allegorically are Jerome (347–420), Augustine (354-430), Gregory of Nyssa (335-394), Cyril of Alexandria (376–444), Gregory of Elvira (359-385), Aponius, Cyril of Jerusalem (313–386), Nilus of Ancyra (d. 430), Hippolytus (222-245), Theodoret of Cyr (393–466).

The Jews believe that the book operates on two levels, the revealed and the concealed.

My interpretation is that the woman is pictured as a Garden Sanctuary - Temple[202]. This woman is the Garden Temple, but also holds the Church inside. The most holy of holies act was God's intimacy in entering a betrothal covenant with creation and His people. In entering the picture of the woman's garden, this intimate act (resembling the act of sex), God breathed light and life into the Garden Temple womb (womb of creation) and from His creative power brought forth His people.

Dinah Dye says in her Book, The Temple Revealed in Creation,

> *"The Creation Covenant is essentially a covenant related to betrothal and marriage."*[203]

Dye, also points to Hosea 2:20-23, which speaks of the Creation Covenant as a betrothal ritual that will be restored, which implies there must have been one from the start.

> *"When that day comes, I will make a covenant for them with the wild animals, the birds in the air and the*

---

[202] Dinah Dye says, Eden, the garden sanctuary, was the original undefiled bride, p.181
[203] Dye, p.18

creeping things of the earth. I will break bow and sword, sweep battle from the land and make them lie down securely. I will betroth you to me forever; yes, I will betroth you to me in righteousness, in justice, in grace and in compassion; I will betroth you to me in faithfulness, and you will know Adonai. When that day come, I will answer, says Adonai I will answer the sky and it will answer the earth." (Hosea 2:20-23).

When God's people, His Church were brought forth in the womb of God, we entered an eternal betrothal covenant in the Garden Temple. The Church, the Bride, in the Woman, the Garden Temple.

As we have seen in previous chapters, the middle of the earth was seen as a cave, a womb. Also, in the first chapter of Genesis, the Hebrew word for 'land' (aretz) is feminine. As God's light shone on the waters upon the earth, they withdrew letting seed come forth, this is describing the waters of the womb bursting. Jewish tradition also says the Garden Temple was like a palace, a womb. For we know that all creation has been groaning in pains of childbirth (Rom 8:22). All these images point to creation looking like a woman.

The term "mother" means home, the centre of the Cosmos. The words mother and matter (creation) also come from the same linguistic roots. We are also told that Jerusalem above is free, and is our mother (Gal 4:26). Many pagan religions know this truth too, they call the earth, mother earth, or womb of Gaia.[204]

Dye, goes on to say, 'In the Song of Songs, the Temple is compared to Solomon's bride being prepared for her wedding

---

[204] Mother earth is a personification of creation, with a particular focus on the nurturing and life-giving aspects of the natural world.

day. She is a young virgin daughter, a beautifully decorated Temple. Her cheeks are adorned with light and her neck showcases a string of luminescent beads. On her arms dangle ornaments of gold and spangles of silver (1.10,11). The bride is black and beautiful, displaying her sun darkened skin that resembles the hides covering the tents of Kedar (1.5). Solomon wrote, 'I have come into my garden, my sister, my bride' (1.5) and 'You are beautiful my darling, like Tirza, lovely as Jerusalem' (6.4). His Bride was also the Tabernacle, likened to a garden sanctuary in the wilderness, the place where God dwelled in the midst of His people. 'How lovely are your tents, O Jacob, and your dwellings, O Israel. (Num 24.5,6).[205]

As above in the heavenly sanctuary of the creation womb, the pattern flows to the tents of the earth. Even a man's wife was considered a house.

God made a marriage covenant with creation, and with His chosen people.

> *"Now may the God of peace who brought up our Lord Jesus from the dead, that great Shepherd of the sheep, through the blood of the everlasting covenant. (Hebrews 13:20)*

> *"But we are bound to give thanks to God always for you, brethren beloved by the Lord, because God from the beginning chose you for salvation through sanctification by the Spirit and belief in the truth." (2 Thessalonians 2:13)*

> *"In hope of eternal life which God, who cannot lie, promised before time began." (Titus 1:2)*

---

[205] Dye, The Temple Revealed in The Garden, Foundations of Torah Publishing, 2015, p. 73

The Church Father Cyprian (250 AD), says, that the Church was sealed in the Garden as the apples on the trees. We were inside the Garden, we are the well-watered trees, and are free to renter when we are born again.

> *"But neither must we pass over what has been necessarily remarked by you, that the Church, according to the Song of Songs, is a garden enclosed, and a fountain sealed, a paradise with the fruit of apples."*

> *"But that the Church is one, the Holy Spirit declares in the Song of Songs, saying, in the person of Christ, 'My dove, my undefiled, is one; she is the only one of her mother, she is the choice one of her that bare her.'* *"Concerning which also He says again, 'A garden enclosed is my sister, my spouse; a spring sealed up, a well of living water.' But if the spouse of Christ, which is the Church, is a garden enclosed; a thing that is closed up cannot lie open to strangers and profane persons. And if it is a fountain sealed, he who, being placed without has no access to the spring, can neither drink thence nor be sealed. And the well also of living water, if it is one and the same within, he who is placed without cannot be quickened and sanctified from that water of which it is only granted to those who are within to make any use, or to drink."*

> *'Under the apple tree I roused you; there your mother conceived you, there she was who in labour gave you birth' (Song of Solomon 8:5)*

Kathleen O'Connor in her Book, 'The Wisdom Literature', says,

INTERPRETATIONS

> *"The song also serves as a metaphor for Wisdom's relationship with human beings. To live with Wisdom, to pursue her and to be pursued by her, is to enter into a love affair set in a garden of paradise where true human desires will be realized. It is a relationship which itself expresses the harmony and blessedness of the universe."*[206]

The Church was birthed in the Garden, and in this Garden womb they experienced God's love and the love of each other in the fullness of the creation Temple. Knowing what we know, this fits perfect with the Jewish idea of a "Tree of Souls" in the Garden. When the fruit fell off the Tree (souls) they were independent spirits, and when they came to earth, their seed produced more trees.[207]

> *"The righteous shall flourish like a palm tree, He shall grow like a cedar in Lebanon. Those who are planted in the house of the Lord shall flourish in the courts of our God." (Psalm 92:12-13)*

> *'Blessed is the man who trust in the Lord, and whose hope is the Lord. For he shall be like a tree planted by the waters, which spreads out its roots by the river." (Jeremiah 17:7-8)*

The Odes of Solomon 11:16, 24 refers to those who are presently identified with the blessing of the trees of Paradise.

---

[206] Kathleen O'Connor, The Wisdom Literature, Wilmington, 1988, p.82
[207] We came out of God, created from His light and sat in the bosom of the Tree of Life, the Tree of Souls (Treasury). Then we growed in Eden and went to the council.

Psalms of Solomon 14:2 also affirms that the Lord's Paradise, the trees of life, are his devout ones.

I believe my interpretation is clear once one has taken all the material into consideration.

CHAPTER 20 - THE MATRIX

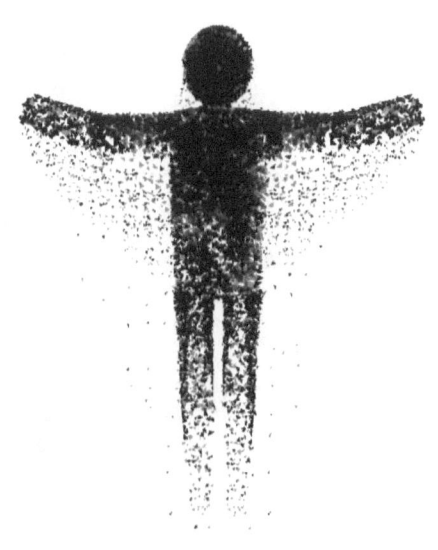

In the Bible interesting enough we do find the word "Matrix", and it does connect in many ways to the film "The Matrix"[208]. The word "Matrix", in the Bible in the Hebrew & Greek means a womb, a birthing channel, a mother's womb. As we have seen in reading this book, creation is a womb, a birthing channel we came into existence from and lived in - out of God. We came out of God into the heavenly sanctuary womb, and then at our appointed time, we were sent, and entered into the earthly womb of creation through a portal (birthing channel - doors of the firmament[209]), and into our mother's womb to be born into the world. There are three main birthing channels, (1) the heavenly sanctuary, (2) the coming down (journey of descent) into the creation realm's (earthly realm), and (3) then, into our mothers birthing channel (womb) to be born.[210]

In the film, The Matrix, one finds themselves in a prison world of slavery (Heb 2:15 - Gal 5:1), seeing dimly to true reality[211]. It is kind of like being in an illusion in the sense of not having knowledge of a higher understanding of what's going on in the world, and our battle for our true identity. Seeing dimly like in a mirror, the Bible has the perfect interpretation (1 Cor

---

[208] The Matrix conveys the idea of a false world of nothing but perceptions. based on the premise that reality is a dream controlled by malevolent forces.
[209] The Book of Enoch, speaks of twelve portals - "And at the end of the earth I saw twelve portals open to all the quarters (of the heaven) from which the winds go forth and blow on the earth." (1 Enoch 76:1).
[210] You could say that there are (4), as the mind is a womb of ideas, which births narratives and perceptions.
[211] I am not saying the Matrix is a Christian film, I'm not trying to relate every point to connect. I'm saying there are some points, references we can take from it. The messiah figure, Neo, and how he had to be incarnate in the matrix, how he was chosen, how he supposedly laid down his life, and how he came back to life to triumph. The biblical names like the hero, Trinity, who loves the messiah back to life. The new birth experience (being unplugged). Being in a world that is veiled, in slavery, seeing dimly. The Bible using the word Matrix as a womb. Some might say the film is to violent, but Jesus when he comes again will fight enemies with his sword and blood spilling (Rev 19:15)

13:12) telling us we need our minds transformed. Even the philosopher Plato had an understanding of the Matrix in his philosophy of the cave, that being, we only see in shadows of true reality[212]. This is what the Bible talks about, being born into a world where we see dimly because of the veil and also because of the fallen structure of the world, which lies under the power of the devil (1 John 5:19). When we are sent into the world, the fallen Matrix (world) wraps itself around our spirit shutting down our true identity, and plugs us into the system. The world is full of false narratives and control, conditioning our minds to live in its stories. Our DNA is continually being manipulated and reprogrammed, of which we must untether from.

The fallen Matrix world is like a womb we feed off, and absorb it's frequencies like connected to an umbilical cord.[213]

> *"Beware lest anyone cheat you through philosophy and empty deceit, according to the traditions of men, according to the basic principles of the world, and not according to Christ." (Colossians 2:8)*

Many are living in a dream, that they need to awake from to see true reality and come into the light. For the true Kingdom is not of this world.

---

[212] Plato said to Socrates in his work 'Phaedo', 'Your favourite doctrine, Socrates, that knowledge is simply recollection, if true, also necessarily implies a previous time in which we have learned that we now recollect. But this would be impossible unless our soul has been in some place existing in the form of man, here then is another proof of the souls immortality.'

[213] The umbilical cord **connects the baby to the mother's placenta**. During fetal development in the womb, the umbilical cord is the lifeline to the baby supplying nutrients and information and frequencies.

> *"Awake, you who sleep, Arise from the dead, And Christ will give you light." (Ephesians 5:14)*[214]

It is only when we are born again that we come into the light, and are led by the Spirit of God that we gain higher understanding of ourselves. Even Jesus said, that he came into the world, and the world did not comprehend him, he came to his own and they didn't receive him (John 1:11). In their fallen state they could not remember or receive the light of truth because of their spiritual damaged state.

> *"But even if our gospel is veiled, it is veiled to those who are perishing, whose minds the god of this age has blinded, who do not believe, lest the light of the gospel of the glory of Christ, who is the image of God, should shine on them." (2 Corinthians 4:4)*

We find the word, Matrix in a number of Passages,

Exodus 13:12: *"That thou shalt set apart unto the LORD all that openeth the matrix, and every firstling that cometh of a beast which thou hast; the males shall be the LORD'S."*

Exodus 13:15: *"And it came to pass, when Pharaoh would hardly let us go, that the Lord slew all the firstborn in the land of Egypt, both the firstborn of man, and the firstborn of beast: therefore, I sacrifice to the LORD all that openeth the **matrix**, being males; but all the firstborn of my children I redeem."*

Exodus 34:19: *"All that openeth the matrix is mine; and every firstling among thy cattle, whether ox or sheep, that is male."*

Numbers 3:12: *"And I, behold, I have taken the Levites from among the children of Israel instead of all the firstborn that*

---

[214] This passage is speaking about people in the world who are alive, but live as if they are dead to reality, they need to be awakened, to awake from the dream.

openeth the matrix among the children of Israel: therefore, the Levites shall be mine...."

Numbers 18:15: *"Everything that openeth the matrix in all flesh, which they bring unto the LORD, whether it be of men or beasts, shall be thine: nevertheless, the firstborn of man shalt thou surely redeem, and the firstling of unclean beasts shalt thou redeem."*

The Hebrew word is *"rehem,"* translated "womb" some 21 times (Genesis 20:18; Genesis 29:31; Genesis 30:22; Exodus 13:2; Numbers 8:16; Numbers 12:12; 1 Samuel 1:5-6; Job 3:11; Job 10:18; Job 24:20; Job 31:15 [x2]; Job 38:8; Psalm 22:10; Psalm 58:3; Psalm 110:3; Jeremiah 1:5; Jeremiah 20:17-18; Hosea 9:14).

In our study we will pick up on Jeremiah 1:5, which speaks of us being known before we came into our mother's womb. "Before I formed you in the womb I knew you, before you were born, I sanctified you. I ordained you a prophet to the nations." This verse is clear we were known by God before we came to earth, even ordained before we were born. The word 'knew' here is the same word used of Adam and Eve knowing each other intimately. It is not just knowing about one with knowledge, but of God knowing us intimately in present form. We were with God before we were born, and there are many young children that do remember their time in heaven before they were born.

I have heard of a Christian Missionary[215], who reports of a heavenly encounter of seeing the revelation of a place where flicking lights, like little candles were beaming together. Out of this mass of flicking lights near the throne, voices were heard

---

[215] I was told about this Missionary from a Pastor I know.

crying out, "send me, send me, send me for your glory". These little lights were pre-existent souls waiting to come to earth.[216]

Melissa Denyce, describes in, 'Soul Before Birth - A Documentary on Pre-Birth Memories', of being in an ocean atmosphere, in waves of love, in a whirlwind cloud of light with God in heaven. In this place were many beings of light (souls). She says we came out of God's love and we are beings of love. She also says that in her experience, she could make some choices in the plan of her life before she was sent to earth.

> "And the temple of God was opened in heaven, and was seen the Ark of His Testament and there were lightening's and voices and thundering." (Revelation 11:10)[217]

> "And out of the throne proceeded lightening's and thundering and voices." (Revelation 4:5)

Dr. Elisabeth Kubler-Ross, a physician from Switzerland is a pioneer of near-death studies. She was nominated for the Nobel Peace Prize. In her studies she has researched thousands of stories, but what is more interesting for us here is the many stories she has researched about young children remembering their time in heaven before they came to earth.

> "People associate me with studies on death, but I have also dealt with thousands of children in my career. Many of them have memories of their spiritual life in heaven before birth. Their parents and others need to listen to them. Young children have much to teach us, but by the age of five or six when they enter school, they

---

[216] 'The spirit of a man is the lamp of the Lord' (Prov 20:27)
[217] A thought to reflect on, are the 'voices' souls waiting in the Ark of the Testimony?

> *become what I call "earth bound" and their memories and connections to heaven fade."*[218]

Dr. Wayne Dyer in his Book, Astounding Recollections of Heaven from Children, reveals a story,

> *At the age of five, my younger son announced out of the blue that he had chosen my wife and me to be his parents. Intrigued, my wife asked how he had done this. He matter-of-factly stated that while he was in heaven before he was born, he had been allowed to go through one door to pick his parents, and through another door to select his brothers and sisters. We were not churchgoers, and have no knowledge of his having obtained this idea from any external source.*
>
> – Robert J. Rinne Orthez, France.[219]

Some may say, but I'm not sure these people are 100 percent Christian, or "oh this author believes other concepts as well". But even if this was true, this does not discredit all their research, as if for example; a Hindu believer can't fix cars or have a degree in science because all his concepts are not Christian. People are on a journey, and if they experience stories of children who recall memories of heaven in their research then we should be open to trusting their findings. Like every story, it is just part (another angle) of a larger amount of evidence gathered in making a case.[220]

---

[218] Meridian magazine, December, 2022
[219] https://www.drwaynedyer.com/blog/5-astounding-recollections-of-heaven-from-children/
[220] In my explaining, note that Dr. Wayne Dyer was not a Hindu, I was just making an example.

Sarah Hinze in her Books, 'The Announcing Dream, Memories of Heaven', and 'Waiting in the Wings', gives a number of children's recollections of their time in heaven.[221]

My Angel Blessed Me

* Rami (age 8) *Before I came to earth, my angel blessed me. She told me I would be having a good mother and father and then a sister too. She said I would do something special on earth, but she didn't say what it was. I felt happy and excited to come to earth. I felt a drop sad to leave my heaven friends, but I knew I could come back [to heaven] in my sleep to visit. My angel hugged me and gave me a lot of love, and told me to give the love to lots of people to make them happy. She said that she would stay close to me and I could talk to her if I needed help.*

The Lady Angel Showed Me My Parents

* Becky (about age 10) *I was scared by the thought of leaving heaven. A woman who looked about thirty came to my rescue. She'd finished her earth life, and knew what mortality was like, because she'd been through it. She reassured me that I would be okay. I had known her for a long time in heaven, even before she went to earth. She was very kind to me and I knew she loved me. This lady angel showed me a future scene of my earthly mother and how proudly my father held me as a newborn. They were beaming, proud parents.*

---

[221] Sarah Hinze, The Announcing Dream: Dreams and Visions About Children Waiting to be Born, Three Orchard Productions, 2016.

It was obvious that they loved me–even needed me to be a part of their lives. Feeling of their love fortified my courage and eased my fear of leaving heaven. I then knew my time on earth would be okay.[222]

This is Where You are Going to Live

* Lisa (when age 4) *One day when I was about four years old, my mother sent me to play outside so she could get some housework done. As I played, I glanced up and looked at the mountain ranges near our farm. It seemed that I had seen those mountains before, but from a different perspective. As I studied them, a vision opened in my mind. I saw myself with a group of boys and girls sitting in a circle on the ground. I didn't count the exact number, but it was about twenty-five or thirty children. I had the impression we were learning, like in school. Suddenly, from behind me and over my right shoulder, I felt my name being called. I say felt because it wasn't a verbal sound–I just knew. I turned and saw a rather tall, slender man standing there. I looked at him and mentally asked, "Is it my time to go?" "Yes," he replied. The next thing I knew, the man and I were moving across the sky above the mountains by our farm. He was on my right side, and we spoke with each other as we went. Suddenly we stopped mid-flight. Looking down, I saw a farmhouse, a barnyard with a fence, a canal behind the house, and a small road winding down a hill. I asked my guide, "Is this where I am going to live?" "Yes!" "Will I be the only child?" "No,*

---

[222] Jewish tradition does believe in female angels. There is one that is called Lailah, the angel of conception, who is like a midwife to souls. Yalkut Hadash (Mal. 63 and 93) says, 'It is appropriate to distinguish between male and female angels.' There are also mermaid angels in heaven as well.

you will be one of many." "Will I be happy there?" "If you want to be." A snowflake fluttered across my eyes, bringing me back to the present. I was born on that farm, and it looked just like it had from the sky. I was the eleventh and last child of the family.

In a number of accounts, I have read, some can choose their parents and in other's they don't. We can kind of see how a new understanding of predestination[223] unfolds.[224] There is God's perfect plan, of which we can weave some of our choices, discussions, agreements into the plan. While also agreeing to walking by trust and faith in God's hidden plans of goodness as well.

As we have mentioned before, Jewish tradition, Jewish Theology understands these stories, 'God sits in a circle with many baby spirits that are about to be born. God knows that the babies won't experience the same joy on earth that they experienced in heaven, and He doesn't want them to be dissatisfied. So, God touches His finger just below their noses, leaving an indentation on their upper lips. This makes them forget the joys

---

[223] "When the number is completed which he had predetermined in His own counsel, all those who have been enrolled for life will rise again. So the number of mankind, corresponding to the fore-ordination of God, will be completed." (Irenaeus 180 AD)

[224] I have been considering the idea that once souls have been ordained in the Council, did some renege on their alliance, but did not birth the desire (Jam 1;15) in heaven, but it was noted. If pre-existence is a fact then is election based on anything in a person's (soul) will? Before they had done anything good or bad in the earth, election stands (Rom 9:11). Were all (many) called (ordained with purpose/function), but few chosen in heaven to be in Christ? The Grace that was given in eternity; was in being chosen in Christ, that being the few that would be saved out of their fallen natures on the earth. It is not because of their works, but faith in agreement from eternity. At this stage, my study of the Scriptures is that it is not clear enough to make a conclusion.

of heaven, so that they can adapt to the world into which they are born.[225]

I read an account about some parents that had two children. 'One child was very young, not even school age yet, the other child was a baby. One night, one of the parents heard the older child in the baby's bedroom, taking to the baby. The parent was concerned and stopped to listen, only to hear the child say, 'Tell me what heaven is like, I'm starting to forget.'[226]

It seems that some children can remember glimpses of heaven, while most of us don't as Jewish tradition describes. Does God allow a few to remember to bring clues of revelation into the world, but this revelation fades quickly? Is this revelation going to become more common as the greater revealing of the sons of God take place?

Creation is a great theatre we are sent into on a stage, to live out a drama, a transforming journey. The drama is real and has eternal consequences if you do not have the true script, the true story, the true interpretation of reality. Without the true script you are living an illusion of who you really are, and are held in bondage.

> *Morpheus : I'm trying to free your mind, Neo. But I can only show you the door. You're the one that has to walk through it.*[227] *(The Matrix)*

> *John 10:9-10* **says***, "**I** am the **door**. If anyone enters by me,* **he** *will be saved and will go in and out and find pasture.*

---

[225] Howard Schwartz, Tree of Souls, The Mythology of Judaism, Oxford University Press, 2004, p 140
[226] fromhispresence.com
[227] In a sense Neo, had to go through the veil back to the Father.

Jesus said of himself, "I am the Way, the Truth (true interpretation) and the Life" (John 14:6) the master composer of the drama. When the final curtain of time is pulled down, men and women, and children from every tongue and tribe will be present before God and will be accountable.

CHAPTER 21 - ORIGEN QUOTES

Throughout this book I have restrained from quoting from the Church Father Origen. I have done this because many, when they hear of his name, turn off, and just call him a heretic. But Origen was in fact a great Theologian, but did sway off into some strange doctrines in his later years. There is a number of his ideas that I totally reject, especially his mutilating of his flesh to try to cut out sin, and his idea of universal redemption (as many claim he taught)[228]. But one thing Origen stood strong on was the doctrine of the pre-existence of the soul, and the rejection of reincarnation. It would be wrong to end this book, without letting Origen speak,

Quotes from Origen, (225 AD),[229]

> *"The world is itself called an 'age,' and it is said to be the conclusion of many ages. Now, the holy apostle teaches that in the age that preceded this one, Christ did not suffer."*

> *"When the Scriptures are carefully examined regarding Jacob and Esau, it is not found to be unrighteous of God to have said, before they were born, or had done anything in this life, that 'the older will serve the younger'. However, it is not unrighteous if we feel that Jacob was worthily beloved by God according to the deserts of his previous life. Owing to causes that have previously existed, a different office is prepared by the*

---

[228] More recent scholars have argued that Origen did not teach universalism, it was more a wish, and he doubted the devil would be restored. Henri Crouzel shows in his research (1) that Origen both affirmed and did not affirm universal reconciliation, which makes it confusing, (2) that he saw that the latter contradicts free will, (3) that wickedness in fallen humanity and fallen angels probably becomes their nature from which free will cannot separate them, and (4) that he could only 'hope' for universal reconciliation because of God's goodness.

[229] In quoting Origen, I am not stating that I hold or agree to his interpretations exactly.

Creator for each one in proportion to the degree of his merit"

"It appears to me that this will be seen more clearly at last if each being, whether heavenly, earthly, or infernal is said to have the causes of his diversity in himself, prior to his bodily birth. There is no doubt that at the Day of Judgment, the good will be separated from the bad (and the just from the unjust) and all will be distributed according to their deserts, by the sentence of God. Similarly, I am of the opinion that such a state of things was the case in the past."

"This is the objection which they generally raise; They say, 'If the world had its beginning in time, what was God doing before the world began? I say that God did not begin to work for the first time when he made this visible world. Just as there will be another world after its destruction, so I believe that other worlds existed before the present one came into being. And both of these positions will be confirmed by the authority of Holy Scripture. That before this world others also existed is shown by Ecclesiastes, in the words, 'Who will speak and say, 'Look! This is new? It has already been in the worlds that have been before us (Eccles 1:9, 10)"[230]

"There has been a descent from a higher to a lower condition on the part of certain souls. This is true not only of those souls who have deserved the change by the variety of their movement but also those who (in order to serve the whole world) were brought down

---

[230] "Spoken to us by His Son, whom He has appointed heir of all things, through whom also He made the worlds." (Hebrews 1:2).

from those higher and invisible spheres to these lower and visible ones, although against their will."[231]

"There was a man sent from God, whose name was John. John was sent from either heaven or paradise or from some other region to this place on earth. But there is a more convincing argument for the view that John was sent from another region when he entered into the body. John was filled with the Holy Spirit even from his mother's womb. This must necessarily assume that John's soul was older than his body, and subsisted by itself before it was sent on the ministry of the witness of the light."

"Referring to John the Baptist - In this place, it does not seem to me that by the word "Elijah" the soul is being spoken of. Otherwise, I would fall into the doctrine of transmigration, which is foreign to the church of God. It is not handed down by the apostles, nor is it set forth in the Scriptures anywhere."[232]

"If the soul of a man, was not formed along with his body, but is proved to have been implanted strictly from without, much more must this be the case with those living beings which are called heavenly. How could his soul and its image be formed along with his body, who, before he was created in the womb, is said to be known to God, and was sanctified by Him before his birth?"[233]

As I have said, in quoting Origen, I am not saying, I interpret or hold exactly to his thoughts, but I point out that he did grasp

---

[231] Against their will is a strange 'term', maybe he means a soul fears at first to leave its perfect home in Heaven, to take the journey of life seeing dimly in the earth.
[232] Origen here rejects reincarnation and the transmigration of souls.
[233] Quotes taken from David Bercot, 'A Dictionary of Early Christian Beliefs'. p.489

the idea of pre-existence. He starts to go wrong in my opinion, when he describes the fall from heaven of all created "beings", and says some of us became angels. This again is the mistake of which I have addressed in the book, we are like, similar, have celestial flesh, but we are not angels. We did not fall and some became angels, we were made a little lower than the angels, not from a fall, but from a perfect design from God.

Origen's interesting take, but a mistake,

> "Although endowed with goodness, these creatures did not possess their goodness as an essential quality. They would only continue to enjoy the blessing of God if they remained good. But they also possessed free will, which they could use to go against God. This abuse of freedom became the case, 'They neglected and despise such goodness, then each one, by fault of his own laziness, became one more quickly, another more slowly, one to a greater degree, another to a lesser degree the cause of his own downfall. The actual visible world became the home of fallen beings, that is, beings who had fallen in the invisible spiritual world. Those who had fallen the least became embodied as angels. Those who had fallen the most became embodied as demons, with Satan as their head. And those who had fallen to an intermediate degree became embodied as human beings. Thus, human beings consist of a soul that fell in a pre-mortal, invisible universe, and a material body." [234]

I'm open to the idea that some 'souls' reneged their alignment in heaven, but didn't birth it (James 1:15)[235], which has

---

[234] Gregg Allison, Historical Theology, p.326.
[235] John Piper, says of James 1:13-15, "But each person is tempted when he is

played out in the doctrine of predestination and election in Christ from eternity. This idea, is just that, and one would have to address a number of passages to fit it all together.[236]

There are only about three main options,

* Pre-existence - God shapes & separates in eternity souls and predestines them by His sovereign choice without a soul's influence.

* Pre-existence - God shapes & separates in eternity souls and predestines them from His sovereign choice & grace from the souls (alignment of their will) alignment in heaven. God's grace chooses/covers them in Christ to be redeemed from the damage of sin that will unfold in the earth, which they can't save themselves from.[237]

* God shapes & separates in eternity in His mind only, and creates souls in bodies in the earth due to His sovereign choice, deciding who will be saved.

There are many questions still to be reflected on, and many passages to be studied, so maybe this will lead to a "Volume Two" to be written. This would focus on the journey of salvation and these ideas, and concepts that follow.

---

lured (exelkomenos) and enticed (deleazomenos) by his own desire. Then desires when it has conceived (syllabousa) gives birth (tiktei) to sin, and sin when it is fully grown brings forth death." - Is to say, that 'tempt' is defined in verse 14 as being 'dragged away and lured.

[236] I have been somewhat of a Calvinist most my life, and I know they are the masters of the Scriptures. But my eyes are seeing a new interpretation.

[237] God foresaw the fall and planned the earth to be a testing ground. We must also remember the power of the fall, that is, None who have been chosen in Christ in eternity, can come to Him (the Son) while on earth unless the Father draws them (John 6:44), and awakens them with new birth. God's grace is that He plans and empowers us to be saved and transformed for His glory. God is saving a world out of a fallen world (Rev 5:9).

Could this be what happened?

* All were brought forth from God,

* All stood before the throne in the Sanctuary,

* All leave, and enter the councils and then into Eden.

* An Angelic up-rise takes place,

* Alignments of souls throughout all nations, tribes, stir in heaven.

* A separation takes place, those who's souls have kept alignment (some out of all nations) in the light, are divided to the right, into Christ, and his secret place. Chosen to be sent, and later glorified in heaven.

* All other souls in all other nations that moved out of alignments are divided to the left into regions of Eden (still in beautiful places).

* All are given the right to come to earth and be tested and merited on their deeds done in the flesh. But there will be many degrees, regions, and places in hell[238] according to layers of one's sinfulness for those on the left.[239]

---

[238] Jesus also warns that the more knowledge that one receives and rejects on earth, and the more intense the evil of their sins (as a whole), the more severe the punishment (Luke 12:42-8; Mark 12:38-40). I believe there will be degrees of dwelling places, in that dark place, even cities.

[239] Could we say, that in the end, ones, destiny is based on one's eternal choices/alignments, from the start, with/from full knowledge?

BIBLIOGRAPHY

Altar, R. (2011) *The Wisdom Books, Job, Proverbs, and Ecclesiastes,* W. W. Norton & Company.

Allison, G. (2011) *Historical Theology; Introduction to Christian Doctrine,* Zondervan Publishing.

Bercot, D. (1998), *A Dictionary of Early Christian Beliefs,* Henderickson Publishers Inc.

Bundesen, L. (2019) *The Feminine Spirit, At the Heart of the Bible,* Anamchara Books.

Clayton, I. (2016) *Realms of the Kingdom, Volume Two,* Sons of Thunder Publications.

Callender, D. (2000) *Adam in Myth and History; Ancient Israelite Perspective on the Primal Human,* Eisenbranus.

Cauley, M. (2012) *The Outer Darkness,* Misthological Press.

Cauley, M. (2021) *Redeemed Bodies Versus Glorified Bodies,* Misthological Press.

Craig, W. (2008) *Reasonable Faith, Christian Truth and Apologetics,* Cross-Way.

Copan, P. (2007) *Loving Wisdom, Christian Philosophy of Religion,* Chalice Press.

Dillow, J. (2004) *Intimacy Ignited, Conversations couple to couple,* Nav-Press.

Dye, D. (2015) *The Temple in the Garden, Priest and Kings,* Foundation Torah.

Fellows, R. (2019) *Wilderness Like Eden,* WordWyze Publishing.

Garcia, Z. (2015) *The Book of the Order of the Ancients,* Lulu.com.

Garcia, Z. (2017) *Paradise; Sides of The North and The Mount of Congregation,* Lulu.com.

George, A. (2005) *The Epic of Gilgamesh,* Penguin Classics.

Geisler, N. (2003) *Systematic Theology, Volume Two, God, Creation,* Beathany House.

Heiser, M. (20150 *The Unseen Realm, Recovering the Supernatural Worldview of the Bible.* Lexham Press.

Henderson, R. (2014) *Operating in The Courts of Heaven*, Robert Henderson Ministries.

Kreeft, P. (1992) *Love is Stronger than Death,* Ignatius Press.

Lehman, K. (2008) Sheet Music, Uncovering the Secrets of Intimacy in Marriage, Tyndale.

O'Connor, K. (1988) *The Wisdom Literature*, Wilmington.

Pitre, B. (2014) *Jesus the Bridegroom, The Greatest Love Story Ever Told,* Image New York.

Raphael, S. (2019) *Jewish Views of the Afterlife,* Rowman & Littlefield.

Rigney, D. (2001) *Glory of God revealed,* Its Supernatural.

Schwartz, H. (2009) *Tree of Souls; the Mythology of Judaism,* Oxford University Press.

Williams, Guy. (2009) *The Spirit World in the Letters of Paul the Apostle,* Rupreecht.

Zacharias, R. (20030 *The Kingdom of the Cults,* Beathany House Publishers.

Other books by Richard Fellows, available online or direct from the author – richfellows@hotmail.com

Wilderness Like Eden (2019) ISBN 978-0-648-58830-6

The supernatural appearing of gemstones from Heaven, around the world, is on the increase as faithful Christians worship God and cry out for the joining of Heaven and earth. What is the phenomenon? How is it related to the God of the Bible?

In Wilderness Like Eden, these questions are addressed in the light of God's Heavenly Kingdom intimately clothing Eden, the Bride and the Sons of God – their functions and callings in the earth.

Granny Rainbow Shekinah (2019)
ISBN 978-0-648-58832-0

Throughout history, God has revealed Himself in His creation. In The Garden of Eden, he visited earth in Theophanies in the Old Testament, in the incarnation of Jesus, and also in disguise, after His resurrection and ascension into Heaven. But what of the Holy Spirit, what is His image and likeness? What is the Holy Spirit's "form" and essence as the Spirit of Glory? In Granny Rainbow Shekinah, these questions and more are addressed. Come on a journey as we go behind the veil!

Heaven Through the Eyes of Children (2021)
ISBN 978-0-648-58834-4

When a Theologian encounters Heaven himself, his heart is opened to believe like a child, and is challenged by a small community of children in the jungles of India experiencing visions of Heaven. Hidden in the remote mountains, a remarkable outpouring of the Holy Spirit touched a community and revealed the reality of Jesus and His Kingdom in Heaven.

This is a Theologian's journey of analysing the geographical landscape of Heaven based on their testimonies. From the eyes of children, through the mind of a Theologian, the truth is revealed.

The Father's Garden (2022)
ISBN 978-0-648-58835-1

Following on from his previous book, Heaven through the eyes of Children, Richard Fellows now brings us to a more detailed description of a specific area of Heaven – the Father's Garden.

Based on various accounts of people throughout the ages, we are given insight into areas of Heaven not often explored before. Few people have the privilege of actually going into these areas and being able to come back to our realm and describe them, but more recently, these areas have been made known to us, to encourage us to look forward to the day we will see Father God face to face. Step inside, and journey through the Father's Garden with Richard!

www.ingramcontent.com/pod-product-compliance
Lightning Source LLC
Chambersburg PA
CBHW030254010526
44107CB00053B/1705